THE NEW DAY

STANFORD UNIVERSITY PRESS
STANFORD UNIVERSITY, CALIFORNIA

LONDON: HUMPHREY MILFORD
OXFORD UNIVERSITY PRESS

———

THE MARUZEN-KABUSHIKI-KAISHA
TOKYO, OSAKA, KYOTO, FUKUOKA, SENDAI

THE BAKER & TAYLOR COMPANY
55 FIFTH AVENUE, NEW YORK

THE NEW DAY

CAMPAIGN SPEECHES OF
HERBERT HOOVER
1928

STANFORD UNIVERSITY PRESS
STANFORD UNIVERSITY, CALIFORNIA

INTRODUCTION

THE FACTS of science have compelled new conceptions of government for a civilization which has virtually been made over in the last fifty years. Instead of the simple farm, village, and small seaport social structure of our forefathers we have the intricate, delicately balanced, interdependent economic organization of the present, with its intimate relationships to all peoples in all parts of the world. Human needs, aspirations, passions, and desires have not changed since the Declaration of Independence and the creation of our Constitution. The importance of keeping intact the rights of individuals and of developing their duties and responsibilities to society is now paramount.

The Presidential campaign of 1928 was as significant as that of 1860. Not since the Lincoln-Douglas debates has the country followed the issues of a campaign with more intensity. The speeches of Mr. Hoover were measured statements of a new liberalism facing new conditions with courage and with confidence in the individual human being to act wisely for himself and for his neighbors. They clarified the citizen's relationship to the great economic mechanism resulting from the practical applications of invention, discovery, and widespread education. These speeches visualized those methods of entering upon the coming constructive period which will lead to equal opportunities for the youth of the United States of America in accordance with their abilities and industry.

The Stanford University Press asked for the privilege of publishing these addresses of Mr. Hoover so that a permanent and authoritative record would be available. Just as his life and deeds have been an inspiration to generations of Stanford men and women, we think that these speeches will stimulate, guide, and hearten the people of our great democracy in the critical and formative years now before us.

RAY LYMAN WILBUR

STANFORD UNIVERSITY
   CALIFORNIA
November 16, 1928

CONTENTS

CHRONOLOGY

HERBERT CLARK HOOVER

1874. Born in West Branch, Cedar County, Iowa, August 10.

1880. Father, Jesse Clark Hoover, died, December 13.

1884. Mother, Huldah Randall (Minthorn) Hoover, died, February 24.

1879–1885. Attended West Branch schools.

1886–1888. Attended Friends' Pacific Academy, Newberg, Oregon.

1888–1891. Office boy, Oregon Land Company, Salem, Oregon.

1891. Entered Stanford University.

1892. Assistant, Arkansas Geological Survey, summer.

1894. Assistant, U. S. Geological Survey, summer.

1895. Granted A.B., in Geology and Mining, Stanford University.

1895. Miner, Nevada County, California.

1896. Assistant to Louis Janin, mining engineer, San Francisco.

1897–1899. Representative in Australia, London mining firm.

1899. Married Miss Lou Henry, A.B., Stanford, 1898, of Monterey, California, February 10.

1899–1901. Representative in China, London mining firm. Active in foreign group during Boxer Rebellion, 1900.

1902–1909. Partner in London mining firm.

1909. Published *Principles of Mining*.

1909–1914. Independent consulting mining engineer, with offices in San Francisco and London.

1912. Published, in collaboration with Lou Henry Hoover, translation of *De Re Metallica* by Georgius Agricola.

1912. Raised money for and built Stanford Union, Stanford University.

1912—. Trustee of Stanford University.

1914. Represented San Francisco, California, in Europe in interests of Panama-Pacific International Exposition. Organized American Relief Committee to aid Americans stranded by the war.

1914–1919. Organized and directed Belgium Relief Commission.

1917–1918. Organized and directed United States Food Administration. Member of War Council, Export Council, Grain Corporation, Sugar Equalization Board.

1919. As American member of Supreme Economic Council directed early relief and economic rehabilitation activities in Europe.

1919–1922. Organized and directed American Relief Administration for aid to destitute children, first in Europe and later throughout Russia.

1920. Founded Hoover War Library at Stanford University; also organized and secured endowment for Food Research Institute, Stanford University. Continued activities for destitute children of Europe and organized C.R.B. Foundation for application of remaining Belgium Relief Commission funds to Belgian education

1921–1928. Secretary of Commerce. Activities directed include: reorganization of Foreign Trade Service; relief of unemployment; elimination of industrial waste; stabilization of construction industries; standardization of materials; development of inland waterways; promotion of commercial aviation; deflation of international rubber market; regulation of radio activities; settlement of war debts; Mississippi flood relief.

1928. Nominated by Republican National Convention at Kansas City, Missouri, as candidate for President of the United States, June 14. Resignation from Cabinet position accepted by President Coolidge, August 21. Elected President, November 6.

THE CONVENTION NOTIFICATION

REPUBLICAN NATIONAL CONVENTION NOTIFIES SECRETARY HOOVER OF NOMINATION

KANSAS CITY, MISSOURI
June 14, 1928

HON. HERBERT HOOVER
2300 S Street Northwest
Washington, D.C.

The Republican National Convention by a sweeping majority, which has since been made unanimous amid great enthusiasm, has named you as its candidate for the Presidency in this campaign. No message of information which I have ever sent to anyone has given me as much satisfaction as this to you. I send it in the name of a united, enthusiastic, and militant party organization, which has turned to you as the inevitable leader in the contest which confronts us. It is not so much that we give you this nomination as that you have earned the right to it. Your training, your equipment, and above all your character make you the leader for whom the party has looked, in order that there may be no halting in the progress of the United States under policies which are warmly approved by the people and to which you have contributed so much. The convention, still in session, would appreciate a message from you and I hope that you may be able speedily to send it to us.

GEORGE H. MOSES

Permanent Chairman
Republican National Convention

SECRETARY HOOVER'S STATEMENT TO THE REPUBLICAN NATIONAL CONVENTION

WASHINGTON, D.C.
June 14, 1928

GEORGE H. MOSES
Chairman Republican National Convention
Kansas City, Missouri

I have your telegram and I sincerely appreciate the confidence which the party has shown in me and the honor bestowed upon me.

You convey too great a compliment when you say that I have earned the right to the presidential nomination. No man can establish such an obligation upon any part of the American people. My country owes me no debt. It gave me, as it gives every boy and girl, a chance. It gave me schooling, independence of action, opportunity for service and honor. In no other land could a boy from a country village, without inheritance or influential friends, look forward with unbounded hope.

My whole life has taught me what America means. I am indebted to my country beyond any human power to repay. It conferred upon me the mission to administer America's response to the appeal of afflicted nations during the war. It has called me into the cabinets of two Presidents. By these experiences I have observed the burdens and responsibilities of the greatest office in the world. That office touches the happiness of every home. It deals with the peace of nations. No man could think of it except in terms of solemn consecration.

You ask me for a message:

A new era and new forces have come into our economic life and our setting among nations of the world. These forces demand of us constant study and effort if prosperity, peace, and contentment shall be maintained.

This convention, like those which have preceded it for two generations, has affirmed the principles of our party and defined its policies upon the problems which now confront us. I stand upon that platform. At a later date I shall discuss it fully, but in the meantime I may well say that under these principles the victory of the party will assure national defense, maintain economy in the administration of government, protect American workmen, farmers, and business men alike from competition arising out of lower standards of living abroad, foster individual initiative, insure stability of business and employment, promote our foreign commerce, and develop our national resources.

You have manifested a deep concern in the problems

of agriculture. You have pledged the party to support specific and constructive relief upon a nation-wide scale backed by the resources of the Federal Government. We must and will find a sound solution that will bring security and contentment to this great section of our people.

But the problems of the next four years are more than economic. In a profound sense they are moral and spiritual. This convention has sounded a note of moral leadership.

Shall the world have peace? Shall prosperity in this nation be more thoroughly distributed? Shall we build steadily toward the ideal of equal opportunity to all our people? Shall there be secured that obedience to law which is the essential assurance of life of our institutions? Shall honesty and righteousness in government and in business confirm the confidence of the people in their institutions and their laws?

Government must contribute to leadership in answer to these questions. The government is more than administration; it is power for leadership and co-operation with the forces of business and cultural life in city, town, and countryside. The Presidency is more than executive responsibility. It is the inspiring symbol of all that is highest in America's purposes and ideals.

It is vital to the welfare of the United States that the Republican Party should continue to administer the

5

government. It is essential that our party should be continued in organization and in strength in order that it may perpetuate its great principles in our national life.

If elected by my fellow-countrymen I shall give the best within me to advance the moral and material welfare of all our people and uphold the traditions of the Republican Party so effectively exemplified by Calvin Coolidge.

HERBERT HOOVER

Formal notice of Herbert Hoover's nomination was brought to him at his Stanford University home by Senator Moses. On the afternoon of August 11 more than 60,000 persons gathered in the Stanford Stadium for the notification ceremonies. California made holiday for the event. On the turf before the speaker's stand bands and drum corps marched. Airplanes flashed overhead, bombarded by rockets and bombs. In front of the platform a battery of microphones, the "ears" of a national hook-up, carried the ceremonies to every radio. Governor C. C. Young introduced Senator Moses, who read to the President-elect the notification of his nomination.

There followed the Address of Acceptance, the first public utterance of the campaign.

ADDRESS OF ACCEPTANCE

August 11, 1928

You bring, Mr. Chairman, formal notice of my nomination by the Republican Party to the Presidency of the United States. I accept. It is a great honor to be chosen for leadership in that party which has so largely made the history of our country in these last seventy years.

Mr. Chairman, you and your associates have in four days traveled three thousand miles across the continent to bring me this notice. I am reminded that in order to notify George Washington of his election Charles Thompson, Secretary of the Congress, spent seven days on horseback to deliver that important intelligence two hundred and thirty miles from New York to Mount Vernon.

In another way, too, this occasion illuminates the milestones of progress. By the magic of the radio this nomination was heard by millions of our fellow-citizens not seven days after its occurrence, nor one day, nor even one minute. They were, to all intents and purposes, present in the hall and participants in the proceedings.

9

Today these same millions have heard your voice and now are hearing mine. We stand in their unseen presence. It is fitting, however, that the forms of our national life, hallowed by generations of usage, should be jealously preserved, and for that reason you have come to me, as similar delegations have come to other candidates through the years.

Those invisible millions have already heard from Kansas City the reading of our party principles. They would wish to hear from me not a discourse upon the platform—in which I fully concur—but something of the spirit and ideals with which it is proposed to carry it into administration.

Nature of Problems Ahead

Our problems of the past seven years have been problems of reconstruction; our problems of the future are problems of construction. They are problems of progress. New and gigantic forces have come into our national life. The Great War released ideas of government in conflict with our principles. We have grown to financial and physical power which compels us into a new setting among nations. Science has given us new tools and a thousand inventions. Through them have come to each of us wider relationships, more neighbors, more leisure, broader vision, higher ambitions, greater problems. To insure that these tools shall not be used to limit liberty has brought a vast array of questions in government.

The points of contact between the government and the people are constantly multiplying. Every year wise governmental policies become more vital in ordinary life. As our problems grow so do our temptations grow to venture away from those principles upon which our republic was founded and upon which it has grown to greatness. Moreover we must direct economic progress in support of moral and spiritual progress.

Our party platform deals mainly with economic problems, but our nation is not an agglomeration of railroads, of ships, of factories, of dynamos, or statistics. It is a nation of homes, a nation of men, of women, of children. Every man has a right to ask of us whether the United States is a better place for him, his wife, and his children to live in, because the Republican Party has conducted the government for nearly eight years. Every woman has a right to ask whether her life, her home, her man's job, her hopes, her happiness will be better assured by the continuance of the Republican Party in power. I propose to discuss the questions before me in that light.

With this occasion we inaugurate the campaign. It shall be an honest campaign; every penny will be publicly accounted for. It shall be a true campaign. We shall use words to convey our meaning, not to hide it.

The Republican Party came into authority nearly eight years ago. It is necessary to remind ourselves of the critical conditions of that time. We were confronted with an incompleted peace and involved in violent and dangerous disputes both at home and abroad. The Federal Government was spending at the rate of five and one-half billions per year; our national debt stood at the staggering total of twenty-four billions. The foreign debts were unsettled. The country was in a panic from overexpansion due to the war and the continued inflation of credit and currency after the Armistice, followed by a precipitant nation-wide deflation which in half a year crashed the prices of commodities by nearly one-half. Agriculture was prostrated; land was unsalable; commerce and industry were stagnated; our foreign trade ebbed away; five millions of unemployed walked the streets. Discontent and agitation against our democracy were rampant. Fear for the future haunted every heart.

No party ever accepted a more difficult task of reconstruction than did the Republican Party in 1921. The record of these seven and one-half years constitutes a period of rare courage in leadership and constructive action. Never has a political party been able to look back upon a similar period with more satisfaction. Never could it look forward with more confidence that its record would be approved by the electorate.

Peace has been made. The healing processes of good will have extinguished the fires of hate. Year by year in our relations with other nations we have advanced the ideals of law and of peace, in substitution for force. By rigorous economy federal expenses have been reduced by two billions per annum. The national debt has been reduced by six and a half billions. The foreign debts have been settled in large part and on terms which have regard for our debtors and for our taxpayers. Taxes have been reduced four successive times. These reductions have been made in the particular interest of the small taxpayers. For this purpose taxes upon articles of consumption and popular service have been removed. The income tax rolls today show a reduction of eighty per cent in the total revenue collected on incomes under $10,000 per year, while they show a reduction of only twenty-five per cent in revenues from incomes above that amount. Each successive reduction in taxes has brought a reduction in the cost of living to all our people.

Commerce and industry have revived. Although the agricultural, coal, and textile industries still lag in their recovery and still require our solicitude and assistance, yet they have made substantial progress. While other countries engaged in the war are only now regaining their pre-war level in foreign trade, our exports, even if we allow for the depreciated dollar, are fifty-eight per cent greater than before the war. Constructive leadership and co-operation by the government have released and stimulated the energies of our people. Faith in the future has been restored. Confidence in our form of government has never been greater.

People's Widening Opportunity

But it is not through the recitation of wise policies in government alone that we demonstrate our progress under Republican guidance. To me the test is the security, comfort, and opportunity that have been brought to the average American family. During this less than eight years our population has increased by eight per cent. Yet our national income has increased by over thirty billions of dollars per year or more than forty-five per cent. Our production—and therefore our consumption —of goods has increased by over twenty-five per cent. It is easily demonstrated that these increases have been widely spread among our whole people. Home ownership has grown. While during this period the number of families has increased by about 2,300,000, we have built more than 3,500,000 new and better homes. In this short time we have equipped nearly nine million more homes with electricity, and through it drudgery has been lifted from the lives of women. The barriers of time and distance have been swept away and life made freer and larger by the installation of six million more telephones, seven million radio sets, and the service of an additional fourteen million automobiles. Our cities are growing magnificent with beautiful buildings, parks, and playgrounds. Our countryside has been knit together with splendid roads.

We have doubled the use of electrical power and with it we have taken sweat from the backs of men. The purchasing power of wages has steadily increased. The hours of labor have decreased. The twelve-hour day has been abolished. Great progress has been made in stabilization of commerce and industry. The job of every man has thus been made more secure. Unemployment in the sense of distress is widely disappearing.

Our Prosperity Wisely Enjoyed

Most of all, I like to remember what this progress has meant to America's children. The portal of their opportunity has been ever widening. While our population has grown but eight per cent, we have increased by eleven per cent the number of children in our grade schools, by sixty-six per cent the number in our high schools, and by seventy-five per cent the number in our institutions of higher learning.

With all our spending we have doubled savings deposits in our banks and building and loan associations. We have nearly doubled our life insurance. Nor have our people been selfish. They have met with a full hand the most sacred obligation of man—charity. The gifts of America to churches, to hospitals, and institutions for the care of the afflicted, and to relief from great disasters have surpassed by hundreds of millions any totals for any similar period in all human record.

One of the oldest and perhaps the noblest of human aspirations has been the abolition of poverty. By poverty I mean the grinding by undernourishment, cold, and ignorance, and fear of old age of those who have the will to work. We in America today are nearer to the final triumph over poverty than ever before in the history of any land. The poorhouse is vanishing from among us. We have not yet reached the goal, but, given a chance to go forward with the policies of the last eight years, we shall soon with the help of God be in sight of the day when poverty will be banished from this nation. There is no guarantee against poverty equal to a job for every man. That is the primary purpose of the economic policies we advocate.

I especially rejoice in the effect of our increased national efficiency upon the improvement of the American home. That is the sanctuary of our loftiest ideals, the source of the spiritual energy of our people. The bettered home surroundings, the expanded schools and playgrounds, and the enlarged leisure which have come with our economic progress have brought to the average family a fuller life, a wider outlook, a stirred imagination, and a lift in aspirations.

Economic advancement is not an end in itself. Successful democracy rests wholly upon the moral and spiritual quality of its people. Our growth in spiritual achievements must keep pace with our growth in physical accomplishments. Material prosperity and moral progress must march together if we would make the United States that commonwealth so grandly conceived by its founders. Our government, to match the expectations of our people, must have constant regard for those human values that give dignity and nobility to life. Generosity of impulse, cultivation of mind, willingness to sacrifice, spaciousness of spirit—those are the qualities whereby America, growing bigger and richer and more powerful, may become America great and noble. A people or government to which these values are not real, because they are not tangible, is in peril. Size, wealth, and power alone cannot fulfill the promise of America's opportunity.

Urgent Need of Farm Relief

The most urgent economic problem in our nation today is in agriculture. It must be solved if we are to bring prosperity and contentment to one-third of our people directly and to all of our people indirectly. We have pledged ourselves to find a solution.

To my mind most agricultural discussions go wrong because of two false premises. The first is that agriculture is one industry. It is a dozen distinct industries incapable of the same organization. The second false premise is that rehabilitation will be complete when it has reached a point comparable with pre-war. Agriculture was not upon a satisfactory basis before the war. The abandoned farms of the Northeast bear their own testimony. Generally there was but little profit in Midwest agriculture for many years except that derived from the slow increases in farm land values. Even of more importance is the great advance in standards of living of all occupations since the war. Some branches of agriculture have greatly recovered, but taken as a whole it is not keeping pace with the onward march in other industries.

There are many causes for failure of agriculture to win its full share of national prosperity. The after-war deflation of prices not only brought great direct losses to the farmer, but he was often left indebted in inflated dollars to be paid in deflated dollars. Prices are often demoralized through gluts in our markets during the harvest season. Local taxes have been increased to provide the improved roads and schools. The tariff on some products is proving inadequate to protect him from imports from abroad. The increases in transportation rates since the war have greatly affected the price which he receives for his products. Over six million farmers in times of surplus engage in destructive competition with one another in the sale of their product, often depressing prices below those levels that could be maintained.

The whole tendency of our civilization during the last fifty years has been toward an increase in the size of the units of production in order to secure lower costs and a more orderly adjustment of the flow of commodities to the demand. But the organization of agriculture into larger units must not be by enlarged farms. The farmer has shown he can increase the skill of his industry without large operations. He is today producing twenty per cent more than eight years ago with about the same acreage and personnel. Farming is and must continue to be an individualistic business of small units and independent ownership. The farm is more than a business: it is a state of living. We do not wish it converted into a mass-production machine. Therefore, if the farmer's position is to be improved by larger operations it must be done not on the farm but in the field of distribution. Agriculture has partially advanced in this direction through co-operatives and pools. But the traditional co-operative is often not a complete solution.

Differences of opinion as to both causes and remedy have retarded the completion of a constructive program of relief. It is our plain duty to search out the common ground on which we may mobilize the sound forces of agricultural reconstruction. Our platform lays a solid basis upon which we can build. It offers an affirmative program.

Bearing of Tariff, Waterways, and Marketing

An adequate tariff is the foundation of farm relief. Our consumers increase faster than our producers. The domestic market must be protected. Foreign products raised under lower standards of living are today competing in our home markets. I would use my office and influence to give the farmer the full benefit of our historic tariff policy.

A large portion of the spread between what the farmer receives for his products and what the ultimate consumer pays is due to increased transportation charges. Increase in railway rates has been one of the penalties of the war. These increases have been added to the cost to the farmer of reaching seaboard and foreign markets and result therefore in reduction of his prices. The farmers of foreign countries have thus been indirectly aided in their competition with the American farmer. Nature has endowed us with a great system of inland waterways. Their modernization will comprise a most substantial contribution to Midwest farm relief and to the development of twenty of our interior states. This modernization includes not only the great Mississippi system, with its joining of the Great Lakes and of the heart of

Midwest agriculture to the Gulf, but also a shipway from the Great Lakes to the Atlantic. These improvements would mean so large an increment in farmers' prices as to warrant their construction many times over. There is no more vital method of farm relief.

But we must not stop here.

An outstanding proposal of the party program is the whole-hearted pledge to undertake the reorganization of the marketing system upon sounder and more economical lines. We have already contributed greatly to this purpose by the acts supporting farm co-operatives, the establishment of intermediate credit banks, the regulation of stockyards and public exchanges, and the expansion of the Department of Agriculture. The platform proposes to go much farther. It pledges the creation of a Federal Farm Board of representative farmers to be clothed with authority and resources with which not only to still further aid farmers' co-operatives and pools and to assist generally in solution of farm problems but especially to build up, with federal finance, farmer-owned and farmer-controlled stabilization corporations which will protect the farmer from the depressions and demoralization of seasonal gluts and periodical surpluses.

Expense No Obstacle

Objection has been made that this program, as laid down by the party platform, may require that several hundred millions of dollars of capital be advanced by the Federal Government without obligation upon the individual farmer. With that objection I have little patience. A nation which is spending ninety billions a year can well afford an expenditure of a few hundred millions for a workable program that will give to one-third of its population their fair share of the nation's prosperity. Nor does this proposal put the government into business except so far as it is called upon to furnish capital with which to build up the farmer to the control of his own destinies.

The program adapts itself to the variable problems of agriculture not only today but which will arise in the future. I do not believe that any single human being or any group of human beings can determine in advance all questions that will arise in so vast and complicated an industry over a term of years. The first step is to create an effective agency directly for these purposes and to give it authority and resources. These are solemn pledges and they will be fulfilled by the Republican Party. It is a definite plan of relief. It needs only the detailed elaboration of legislation and appropriations to put it into force.

During my term as Secretary of Commerce I have steadily endeavored to build up a system of co-operation between the government and business. Under these co-operative actions all elements interested in the problems of a particular industry such as manufacturer, distributor, worker, and consumer have been called into council together, not for a single occasion but for continuous work. These efforts have been successful beyond any expectation. They have been accomplished without interference or regulation by the government. They have secured progress in the industries, remedy for abuses, elimination of waste, reduction of cost in production and distribution, lower prices to the consumer, and more stable employment and profit. While the problem varies with every different commodity and with every different part of our great country, I should wish to apply the same method to agriculture so that the leaders of every phase of each group can advise and organize on policies and constructive measures. I am convinced that this form of action, as it has done in other industries, can greatly benefit farmer, distributor, and consumer.

The working out of agricultural relief constitutes the most important obligation of the next administration. I stand pledged to these proposals. The object of our policies is to establish for our farmers an income equal to those of other occupations; for the farmer's wife the same comforts in her home as women in other groups; for the farm boys and girls the same opportunities in life as other boys and girls. So far as my own abilities may be of service, I dedicate them to help secure prosperity and contentment in that industry where I and my forefathers were born and nearly all my family still obtain their livelihood.

Protective Principle Reaffirmed

The Republican Party has ever been the exponent of protection to all our people from competition with lower standards of living abroad. We have always fought for tariffs designed to establish this protection from imported goods. We also have enacted restrictions upon immigration for the protection of labor from the inflow of workers faster than we can absorb them without breaking down our wage levels.

The Republican principle of an effective control of imported goods and of immigration has contributed greatly to the prosperity of our country. There is no selfishness in this defense of our standards of living. Other countries gain nothing if the high standards of America are sunk and if we are prevented from building a civilization which sets the level of hope for the entire world. A general reduction in the tariff would admit a flood of goods from abroad. It would injure every home. It would fill our streets with idle workers. It would destroy the returns to our dairymen, our fruit, flax, and live-stock growers, and our other farmers.

No man will say that any immigration or tariff law is perfect. We welcome our new immigrant citizens and their great contribution to our nation; we seek only to protect them equally with those already here. We shall amend the immigration laws to relieve unnecessary hardships upon families. As a member of the commission whose duty it is to determine the quota basis under the national origins law I have found it is impossible to do so accurately and without hardship. The basis now in effect carries out the essential principle of the law and I favor repeal of that part of the act calling for a new basis of quotas.

We have pledged ourselves to make such revisions in the tariff laws as may be necessary to provide real protection against the shiftings of economic tides in our various industries. I am sure the American people would rather entrust the perfection of the tariff to the consistent friend of the tariff than to our opponents, who have always reduced our tariffs, who voted against our present protection to the worker and the farmer, and whose whole economic theory over generations has been the destruction of the protective principle.

The Interests of Labor

Having earned my living with my own hands, I cannot have other than the greatest sympathy with the aspirations of those who toil. It has been my good fortune during the past twelve years to have received the co-operation of labor in many directions, and in promotion of many public purposes.

The trade union movement in our country has maintained two departures from such movements in all other countries. They have been staunch supporters of American individualism and American institutions. They have steadfastly opposed subversive doctrines from abroad. Our freedom from foreign social and economic diseases is in large degree due to this resistance by our own labor. Our trade unions, with few exceptions, have welcomed all basic improvement in industrial methods. This largeness of mind has contributed to the advancing standards of living of the whole of our people. They properly have sought to participate—by additions to wages—in the result of improvements and savings which they have helped to make.

During these past years we have grown greatly in the mutual understanding between employer and employee. We have seen a growing realization by the employer that the highest practicable wage is the road to increased consumption and prosperity, and we have seen a growing realization by labor that the maximum use of machines, of effort, and of skill is the road to lower production costs and in the end to higher real wages. Under these impulses and the Republican protective system our industrial output has increased as never before and our wages have grown steadily in buying power. Our workers with their average weekly wages can today buy two and often three times more bread and butter than any wage earner of Europe. At one time we demanded for our workers a "full dinner pail." We have now gone far beyond that conception. Today we demand larger comfort and greater participation in life and leisure.

The Republican platform gives the pledge of the party to the support of labor. It endorses the principle of collective bargaining and freedom in labor negotiations. We stand also pledged to the curtailment of excessive use of the injunction in labor disputes.

Our Waterpower Resources

The war and the necessary curtailment of expenditure during the reconstruction years have suspended the construction of many needed public works. Moreover, the time has arrived when we must undertake a larger-visioned development of our water resources. Every drop which runs to the sea without yielding its full economic service is a waste.

Nearly all of our greater drainages contain within themselves possibilities of cheapened transportation, irrigation, reclamation, domestic water supply, hydro-electric power, and frequently the necessities of flood control. But this development of our waters requires more definite national policies in the systematic co-ordination of those different works upon each drainage area. We have wasted scores of millions by projects undertaken not as a part of a whole but as the consequence of purely local demands. We cannot develop modernized water transportation by isolated projects. We must develop it as a definite and positive interconnected system of transportation. We must adjust reclamation and irrigation to our needs for more land. Where they lie together we must co-ordinate transportation with flood control, the development of hydro-electric power and of irrigation, else we shall as in the past commit errors that will take years and millions to remedy. The Congress has authorized and has in process of legislation great programs of public works. In addition to the works in development of water resources, we have in progress large undertakings in public roads and the construction of public buildings.

All these projects will probably require an expenditure of upward of one billion dollars within the next four years. It comprises the largest engineering construction ever undertaken by any government. It involves three times the expenditure laid out upon the Panama Canal. It is justified by the growth, need, and wealth of our country. The organization and administration of this construction is a responsibility of the first order. For it we must secure the utmost economy, honesty, and skill. These works, which will provide jobs for an army of men, should so far as practicable be adjusted to take up the slack of unemployment elsewhere.

I rejoice in the completion of legislation providing

adequate flood control of the Mississippi. It marks not alone the undertaking of a great national task, but it constitutes a contribution to the development of the South. In encouragement of their economic growth lies one of the great national opportunities of the future.

Stand on Law Enforcement

I recently stated my position upon the Eighteenth Amendment, which I again repeat:

"I do not favor the repeal of the Eighteenth Amendment. I stand for the efficient enforcement of the laws enacted thereunder. Whoever is chosen President has under his oath the solemn duty to pursue this course.

"Our country has deliberately undertaken a great social and economic experiment, noble in motive and far-reaching in purpose. It must be worked out constructively."

Common sense compels us to realize that grave abuses have occurred—abuses which must be remedied. An organized searching investigation of fact and causes can alone determine the wise method of correcting them. Crime and disobedience of law cannot be permitted to break down the Constitution and laws of the United States.

Modification of the enforcement laws which would permit that which the Constitution forbids is nullification. This the American people will not countenance.

Change in the Constitution can and must be brought about only by the straightforward methods provided in the Constitution itself. There are those who do not believe in the purposes of several provisions of the Constitution. No one denies their right to seek to amend it. They are not subject to criticism for asserting that right. But the Republican Party does deny the right of anyone to seek to destroy the purposes of the Constitution by indirection.

Whoever is elected President takes an oath not only to faithfully execute the office of the President, but that oath provides still further that he will, to the best of his ability, preserve, protect, and defend the Constitution of the United States. I should be untrue to these great traditions, untrue to my oath of office, were I to declare otherwise.

The Government and Business

With impressive proof on all sides of magnificent progress, no one can rightly deny the fundamental correctness of our economic system. Our pre-eminent advance over nations in the last eight years has been due to distinctively American accomplishments. We do not owe these accomplishments to our vast natural resources. These we have always had. They have not increased. What has changed is our ability to utilize these resources more effectively. It is our human resources that have changed. Man for man and woman for woman, we are today more capable, whether in the work of farm, factory, or business, than ever before. It lies in our magnificent educational system, in the hard-working character of our people, in the capacity of far-sighted leadership in industry, the ingenuity, the daring of the pioneers of new inventions, in the abolition of the saloon, and the wisdom of our national policies.

With the growth and increasing complexity of our economic life the relations of government and business are multiplying daily. They are yearly more dependent upon each other. Where it is helpful and necessary, this relation should be encouraged. Beyond this it should not go. It is the duty of government to avoid regulation as long as equal opportunity to all citizens is not invaded and public rights violated. Government should not engage in business in competition with its citizens. Such actions extinguish the enterprise and initiative which has been the glory of America and which has been the root of its pre-eminence among the nations of the earth. On the other hand, it is the duty of business to conduct itself so that government regulation or government competition is unnecessary.

Business is practical, but it is founded upon faith—faith among our people in the integrity of business men, and faith that it will receive fair play from the government. It is the duty of government to maintain that faith. Our whole business system would break down in a day if there was not a high sense of moral responsibility in our business world. The whole practice and ethics of business has made great strides of improvement in the last quarter of a century, largely due to the effort of business and the professions themselves. One of the most helpful signs of recent years is the stronger growth of associations of workers, farmers, business men, and professional men with a desire to cure their own abuses and a purpose to serve public interest. Many problems can be solved through co-operation between government and these self-governing associations to improve methods and practices. When business cures its own abuses it is true self-government, which comprises more than political institutions.

Simplification of Contacts Needed

One of the greatest difficulties of business with government is the multitude of unnecessary contacts with government bureaus, the uncertainty and inconsistency of government policies, and the duplication of governmental activities. A large part of this is due to the scattering of functions and the great confusion of responsibility in our federal organization. We have, for instance, fourteen different bureaus or agencies engaged in public works and construction, located in nine different departments of the government. It brings about competition between government agencies, inadequacy of control, and a total lack of co-ordinated policies in public works. We have eight different bureaus and agencies charged with conservation of our natural resources, located in five different departments of the government. These conditions exist in many other directions. Divided responsibility, with the absence of centralized authority, prevents constructive and consistent development of broad national policies.

Our Republican presidents have repeatedly recommended to Congress that it would not only greatly reduce expenses of business in its contacts with government but that a great reduction could be made in governmental expenditure and more consistent and continued national policies could be developed if we could secure the grouping of these agencies devoted to one major purpose under single responsibility and authority. I have had the good fortune to be able to carry out such reorganization in respect to the Department of Commerce. The results have amply justified its expansion to other departments and I should consider it an obligation to enlist the support of Congress to effect it.

Proper Promotion of Business a Government Function

The government can be of invaluable aid in the promotion of business. The ideal state of business is freedom from those fluctuations from boom to slump which

33

bring on one hand the periods of unemployment and bankruptcy and, on the other, speculation and waste. Both are destructive to progress and fraught with great hardship to every home. By economy in expenditures, wise taxation, and sound fiscal finance it can relieve the burdens upon sound business and promote financial stability. By sound tariff policies it can protect our workmen, our farmers, and our manufacturers from lower standards of living abroad. By scientific research it can promote invention and improvement in methods. By economic research and statistical service it can promote the elimination of waste and contribute to stability in production and distribution. By promotion of foreign trade it can expand the markets for our manufacturers and farmers and thereby contribute greatly to stability and employment.

Our people know that the production and distribution of goods on a large scale is not wrong. Many of the most important comforts of our people are only possible by mass production and distribution. Both small and big business have their full place. The test of business is not its size—the test is whether there is honest competition, whether there is freedom from domination, whether there is integrity and usefulness of purpose. As Secretary of Commerce I have been greatly impressed by the fact that the foundation of American business is the independent business man. The Department by encouragement of his associations and by provision of special services has endeavored to place him in a position of equality in information and skill with larger operations. Alike with our farmers his is the stronghold of American individuality. It is here that our local communities receive their leadership. It is here that we refresh our leadership for larger enterprise. We must maintain his opportunity and his individual service. He and the public must be protected from any domination or from predatory business.

Women and the Ballot

I have said that the problems before us are more than economic, that in a much greater degree they are moral and spiritual. I hold that there rests upon government many responsibilities which affect the moral and spiritual welfare of our people. The participation of women in politics means a keener realization of the importance of these questions. It means higher political standards.

One-half of our citizens fail to exercise the responsibilities of the ballot box. I would wish that the women of our country could embrace this problem in citizenship as peculiarly their own. If they could apply their higher sense of service and responsibility, their freshness of enthusiasm, their capacity for organization to this problem, it would become, as it should become, an issue of profound patriotism. The whole plane of political life would be lifted, the foundations of democracy made more secure.

Religious Tolerance

In this land, dedicated to tolerance, we still find outbreaks of intolerance. I come of Quaker stock. My ancestors were persecuted for their beliefs. Here they sought and found religious freedom. By blood and conviction I stand for religious tolerance both in act and in spirit. The glory of our American ideals is the right of every man to worship God according to the dictates of his own conscience.

Corruption

In the past years there has been corruption participated in by individual officials and members of both political parties in national, state, and municipal affairs. Too often this corruption has been viewed with indifference by a great number of our people. It would seem unnecessary to state the elemental requirement that government must inspire confidence not only in its ability but in its integrity. Dishonesty in government, whether national, state, or municipal, is a double wrong. It is treason to the state. It is destructive of self-government. Government in the United States rests not only upon the consent of the governed but upon the conscience of the nation. Government weakens the moment that its integrity is even doubted. Moral incompetency by those entrusted with government is a blighting wind upon private integrity. There must be no place for cynicism in the creed of America.

The Civil Service

Our Civil Service has proved a great national boon. Appointive office, both North, South, East, and West, must be based solely on merit, character, and reputation in the community in which the appointee is to serve; as it is essential for the proper performance of their duties that officials shall enjoy the confidence and respect of the people with whom they serve.

The Young of America

For many years I have been associated with efforts to save life and health for our children. These experiences with millions of children both at home and abroad have left an indelible impression—that the greatness of any nation, its freedom from poverty and crime, its aspirations and ideals are the direct quotient of the care of its children. Racial progress marches upon the feet of healthy and instructed children. There should be no child in America that is not born and does not live under sound conditions of health; that does not have full opportunity of education from the beginning to the end of our institutions; that is not free from injurious labor; that does not have every stimulation to accomplish the fullest of its capacities. Nothing in development of child life will ever replace the solicitude of parents and the surroundings of home, but in many aspects both parents and children are dependent upon the vigilance of government—national, state, and local.

I especially value the contribution that the youth of the country can make to the success of our American experiment in democracy. Theirs is the precious gift of enthusiasm, without which no great deeds can be accomplished. A government that does not constantly seek to live up to the ideals of its young men and women falls short of what the American people have a right to expect and demand from it. To interpret the spirit of the youth into the spirit of our government, to bring the warmth of their enthusiasm and the flame of their idealism into the affairs of the nation—is to make of American government a positive and living force, a factor for greatness and nobility in the life of the nation.

World Peace

I think I may say that I have witnessed as much of the horror and suffering of war as any other American. From it I have derived a deep passion for peace. Our foreign policy has one primary object, and that is peace. We have no hates; we wish no further possessions; we harbor no military threats. The unspeakable experiences of the Great War, the narrow margin by which civilization survived its exhaustion, is still vivid in men's minds.

There is no nation in the world today that does not earnestly wish for peace—that is not striving for peace.

There are two co-operating factors in the maintenance of peace—the building of good will by wise and sympathetic handling of international relations, and the adequate preparedness for defense. We must not only be just; we must be respected. The experiences of the war afforded final proof that we cannot isolate ourselves from the world, that the safeguarding of peace cannot be attained by negative action. Our offer of treaties open to the signature of all, renouncing war as an instrument of national policy, proves that we have every desire to co-operate with other nations for peace. But our people have determined that we can give the greatest real help —both in times of tranquillity and in times of strain—if we maintain our independence from the political exigencies of the Old World. In pursuance of this, our country has refused membership in the League of Nations, but we are glad to co-operate with the League in its endeavors to further scientific, economic, and social welfare, and to secure limitation of armament.

We believe that the foundations of peace can be strengthened by the creation of methods and agencies by which a multitude of incidents may be transferred from the realm of prejudice and force to arbitration and the determination of right and wrong based upon international law.

Defense

We have been and we are particularly desirous of furthering the limitation of armaments. But in the meantime we know that in an armed world there is only one certain guarantee of freedom—and that is preparedness for defense. It is solely to defend ourselves, for the protection of our citizens, that we maintain armament. No clearer evidence of this can exist than the unique fact that we have fewer men in army uniform today than we have in police uniforms, and that we maintain a standing invitation to the world that we are always ready to limit our naval armament in proportion as the other naval nations will do likewise. We earnestly wish that the burdens and dangers of armament upon every home in the world might be lessened. But we must and shall maintain our naval defense and our merchant marine in the strength and efficiency which will yield to us at all times the primary assurance of liberty, that is, of national safety.

The Ideal of Equality

There is one of the ideals of America upon which I wish at this time to lay especial emphasis. For we should constantly test our economic, social, and governmental system by certain ideals which must control them. The founders of our republic propounded the revolutionary doctrine that all men are created equal and all should have equality before the law. This was the emancipation of the individual. And since these beginnings, slowly, surely, and almost imperceptibly, this nation has added a third ideal almost unique to America—the ideal of equal opportunity. This is the safeguard of the individual. The simple life of early days in our republic found but few limitations upon equal opportunity. By the crowding of our people and the intensity and complexity of their activities it takes today a new importance.

Equality of opportunity is the right of every American—rich or poor, foreign or native-born, irrespective of faith or color. It is the right of every individual to attain that position in life to which his ability and character entitle him. By its maintenance we will alone hold open the door of opportunity to every new generation, to every boy and girl. It tolerates no privileged classes or castes or groups who would hold opportunity as their prerogative. Only from confidence that this right will be upheld can flow that unbounded courage and hope which stimulate each individual man and woman to endeavor and to achievement. The sum of their achievement is the gigantic harvest of national progress.

Not Socialism

This ideal of individualism based upon equal opportunity to every citizen is the negation of socialism. It is

41

the negation of anarchy. It is the negation of despotism. It is as if we set a race. We, through free and universal education, provide the training of the runners; we give to them an equal start; we provide in the government the umpire of fairness in the race. The winner is he who shows the most conscientious training, the greatest ability, and the greatest character. Socialism bids all to end the race equally. It holds back the speedy to the pace of the slowest. Anarchy would provide neither training nor umpire. Despotism picks those who should run and those who should win.

Conservative, progressive, and liberal thought and action have their only real test in whether they contribute to equal opportunity, whether they hold open the door of opportunity. If they do not they are false in their premise no matter what their name may be.

It was Abraham Lincoln who firmly enunciated this ideal as the equal chance. The Sherman Law was enacted in endeavor to hold open the door of equal opportunity in business. The commissions for regulation of public utilities were created to prevent discrimination in service and prevent extortion in rates—and thereby the destruction of equal opportunity.

Equality of opportunity is a fundamental principle of our nation. With it we must test all our policies. The success or failure of this principle is the test of our government.

Problems Merely Mentioned

Mr. Chairman, I regret that time does not permit the compass of many important questions. I hope at a later time to discuss the development of waterways, highways, aviation, irrigable lands, foreign trade and merchant marine, the promotion of education, more effective administration of our criminal laws, the relation of our government to public utilities and railways, the primary necessity of conservation of natural resources, measures for further economy in government and reduction of taxes—all of which afford problems of the first order.

The Office of President

I would violate my conscience and the gratitude I feel, did I not upon this occasion express appreciation of the great President who leads our party today. President Coolidge has not only given a memorable administration, he has left an imprint of rectitude and statesmanship upon the history of our country. His has been the burden of reconstruction of our country from the destruction of war. He has dignified economy to a principle of government. He has charted the course of our nation and our party over many years to come. It is not only a duty but it is the part of statesmanship that we adhere to this course.

No man who stands before the mighty forces which ramify American life has the right to promise solutions at his hand alone. All that an honest man can say is that, within the extent of his abilities and his authority and in co-operation with the Congress and with leaders of every element in our people, these problems shall be courageously met and solution will be courageously attempted.

Our purpose is to build in this nation a human society, not an economic system. We wish to increase the efficiency and productivity of our country, but its final purpose is happier homes. We shall succeed through the faith, the loyalty, the self-sacrifice, the devotion to eternal ideals which live today in every American.

The matters which I have discussed directly and deeply affect the moral and spiritual welfare of our country. No one believes these aspirations and hopes can be realized in a day. Progress or remedy lie often enough in the hands of state and local government. But the awakening of the national conscience and the stimulation of every remedial agency is indeed a function of the national government. I want to see our government great both as an instrument and as a symbol of the nation's greatness.

The Presidency is more than an administrative office. It must be the symbol of American ideals. The high and the lowly must be seen with the same eyes, met in the same spirit. It must be the instrument by which national conscience is livened and it must under the guidance of the Almighty interpret and follow that conscience.

The little Iowa town where Herbert Hoover was born was the scene of the second campaign address. Mr. Hoover spoke in a huge tent, after a day spent in renewing old acquaintances, visiting boyhood haunts. The population of West Branch is seven hundred and forty-five; but a crowd of from twelve to fifteen thousand, mostly farmers, came from Iowa and Illinois to hear the candidate's home-town address.

WEST BRANCH, IOWA

August 21, 1928

THIS is a homecoming. It hardly seems an occasion for a lengthy political speech—rather is it an opportunity to recall old associations and renew old friendships.

I am glad, a son of Iowa, to come back to the place where I was born. Here I spent the first ten years of my boyhood. Here my parents and my grandparents toiled, worshipped God, did their part in building this community, and now lie in the cemetery over the hill.

During the past forty-four years I have returned from time to time that I might pay respect to their memory, that I might express my appreciation of those kindly and sympathetic folk who, taking a boy to their hearts, wiped away the one grief of childhood. One of my vivid recollections was my earnest interest in the debate between neighbors and relatives when they were discussing not who was to assume me as a burden, but who was to take the boy as a member of their own flock. That is the spirit of the people of Iowa. It is the spirit of the thousands of villages and towns in all this wide land.

And I have no apology for even a more personal note.

There is present here today a lady who took part in that debate and who was for years my teacher in your public school. She embodies the spirit of that vast body of women who not only teach and inspire our children but watch over their wider destinies. You have come to do me courtesy as a son of Iowa. I take this occasion to acknowledge my debt to that lady—Mrs. Curran.

Reminiscences of Boyhood

There is no imprint upon our minds so deep as those of early boyhood. Mine are the joys of Iowa—the glories of snowy winter, the wonder at the growing crops, the joining of the neighbors to harvest, the gathering of apples, the pilgrimage to the river woods for the annual fuel and nuts, the going to school, the interludes from work, in the swimming hole, fishing in creeks, the hunting for prairie chickens and rabbits in the hedges and woods. It is the entry to life which I could wish for every American boy and girl.

Again today I have had refreshment of spirit in returning to these scenes. The swimming hole is still in use. It has the same mudbank. It is still impossible to dress without carrying mud home in one's inner garments. As an engineer I could devise improvements for that swimming hole. But I doubt if the decrease in mothers' grief at the homecoming of muddy boys would compensate the inherent joys of getting muddy.

I have been to see the old Quaker meetinghouse. It has been moved across the street and replaced by a more modern structure. The old building appears at some time to have been turned into a moving-picture house, which reminds me of the time I heard Aunt Hannah, moved in meeting, bitterly denounce the rise of modern ways and prophesy that, if they were persisted in, that edifice dedicated to God would some day be transformed into a place of abomination. I do not place the movies in that class, but knowing Aunt Hannah's views on any form of human recreation, even to the godlessness of sliding down hill, I suspect that if she knew of this she would get great satisfaction at the consummation of her warnings.

This was always a Republican village. It was here that I received my first touch of the national life. I well recollect the hoisting of the flag at half-mast over my father's blacksmith shop on the assassination of President Garfield. I also recollect well the torchlight procession in the Garfield election. I was not high enough to be permitted the conduct of a torch, but I participated by walking alongside for miles. At that time there were two or three Democrats in the town. I do not know today whether what seemed to me an enormous torch-light parade was instituted for their conversion or not, but I believe it was quite hopeless, because one of my boyhood friends and opponents in battle, who I expect

49

is in this audience today, is a descendant of one of those Democrats and has been regenerated only in the last month.

I am proud to have been born in Iowa. I have ofttimes said that the good Lord made it the richest stretch of agricultural land that ever blessed any one sovereign government. It was settled by the adventurous, the courageous, who fought their way across the ever-extending frontier; they have builded here in so short a period as seventy-five years a state with the least poverty, the highest average intelligence, the most generous education which ever blessed a single commonwealth.

An Epitome of American Progress

Here in West Branch can be found all the milestones of the changes which have come to American agriculture. Only a mile from here is the farm of my Uncle Allen, where I spent some years of my boyhood. That was just at the passing stage of the great pioneer movement. Many farms were still places where we tilled the soil for the immediate needs of our families. We ground our wheat and corn on toll at the mill; we slaughtered our hogs for meat; we wove at least a part of our own clothing; we repaired our own machinery; we got our own fuel from the woods; we erected our own buildings; we made our own soap; we preserved our own fruit and grew our own vegetables. Only a small part of the family living came by purchases from the outside. Perhaps twenty per cent of the products were sold in the markets to purchase the small margin of necessities which we could not ourselves produce, and to pay interest on the mortgage.

In a half-century the whole basis of agriculture has shifted. We have improved seed and live-stock; we have added a long list of mechanical inventions for saving of labor; we have increased the productivity of the land. And it has become a highly specialized business. There is no longer one industry called farming, but in fact a dozen industries. Probably over eighty per cent of its products now go directly or indirectly to the markets, and probably over eighty per cent of the family living must be purchased from outside. In the old days when prices fluctuated in the Chicago market, at most they affected only twenty per cent of the income of the farm. A violent drop in prices could reduce the family income by only four or five per cent. Today the same fluctuation in price, affecting as it does eighty per cent to one hundred per cent of the products of the farm, can take twenty-five to fifty per cent away from the family net income and make the difference between comfort and freedom from anxiety or, on the other hand, debts and discouragements.

I do not suggest a return to the greater security which agriculture enjoyed in its earlier days, because with that security were lower standards of living, greater toil, less opportunity for leisure and recreation, less of the comforts of home, less of the joy of living.

I am often conscious of sentimental regret for the passing of those old-time conditions. I have sometimes been as homesick for the ways of those self-contained farm homes of forty years ago as I have been for the kindly folk who lived in them. But I know it is no more possible to revive those old conditions than it is to summon back the relatives and friends in the cemetery yonder. While we recognize and hold fast to what is permanent in the old-time conditions, we must accept what is inevitable in the changes that have taken place. It is fortunate indeed that the principles upon which our government was founded require no alteration to meet these changes.

Just as there is transformation in agriculture, so there is in other industry; just as there is more specialization on the farm, so there is in other industry. We live today by the exchange of goods among ten thousand sorts of producers of specialties. A large number of occupations which were conducted on the farm in old days are now conducted in the factory. That is one reason why we have a decreasing proportion of our people on the farms. By this revolution the American farmer has become enmeshed in powerful, and yet delicate, economic forces, which are working to his disadvantage.

In my acceptance speech ten days ago I made an extended statement upon the legislative proposals for relief to the agricultural industry which the Republican Party has put forward in its platform. You would not wish me to take your time to review that statement. I should, however, like to emphasize that the spirit of those legislative proposals is to work out a more economic and stable marketing system. A Federal Farm Board is to be set up with the necessary powers and resources to assist the industry to meet not alone the varied problems of today, but those which may arise in the future. My fundamental concept of agriculture is one controlled by its own members, organized to fight its own economic battles and to determine its own destinies. Nor do I speak of organization in the narrow sense of traditional farm co-operatives or pools, but in the much wider sense of a sound marketing organization. It is not by these proposals intended to put the government into the control of the business of agriculture, nor to subsidize the prices of farm products and pay the losses thereon either by the federal treasury or by a tax or fee on the farmer. We propose with governmental assistance and an initial advance of capital to enable the agricultural industry to reach a stature of modern business operations by which the farmer will attain his independence and maintain his individuality.

And upon this whole question I should like to repeat from my acceptance speech that:

"The working out of agricultural relief constitutes the most important obligation of the next administration. The object of our policies is to establish for our farmers an income equal to those of other occupations; for the farmer's wife the same comforts in her home as women in other groups; for the farm boys and girls the same opportunities in life as other boys and girls. So far as my own abilities may be of service, I dedicate them to help secure prosperity and contentment in that industry where I and my forefathers were born and nearly all my family still obtain their livelihood."

In formulating recommendations for legislation to carry out the proposals of the party, I trust that we may have the full assistance of the leaders of agricultural thought. I am not insensible to the value of the study which sincere farm leaders have given to this question of farm legislation. They have all contributed to the realization that the problem must be solved. They will be invited into conference. Outstanding farmers such as Governor Lowden will be asked to join in the search for common ground upon which we can act.

Interior Waterways Needed

I had thought today to particularly point out the importance of the development of our interior waterways as bearing on the prosperity not only of agriculture but of the whole of our Midwest business and commerce. It is a most important supplement to agricultural relief. The necessarily large advances in railway rates from the war militate against the economic setting of this whole interior section. This, together with the completion of the Panama Canal and the fact that ocean rates have increased but little since before the war, further disturbs the whole economic relationship of the Midwest. It is as if a row of toll gates had been placed around this whole section of our country. It seriously affects the farmer. I think we can accept it as an economic fact that the farmer on most occasions pays the freight on his products. It is a deduction from the ultimate price; you yourself can attest this. In a general way, the center point of markets is overseas or the Atlantic seaboard, where prices are determined by the meeting of streams of world products. For every hundred miles you are removed from these market centers the price of farm products is lower by the amount of freight rates. Some calculations which I made a few years ago showed that the increases in railway rates had in effect moved the Midwest two hundred to four hundred miles farther from seaboard. Moreover, some of the competitive agricultural regions such as the Argentine and Australia are close to seaboard, and, with sea rates about the same as before the war, they are able to compete with the American farmer in foreign markets to a greater advantage than before the war. This increase in transportation rates also affects the prices of many things which the farmer must buy, for much raw material which comes into the Midwest pays the increased freight rate and this in turn is taken up by the consumer. We cannot return to pre-war railway rates without ruin to the railways. Therefore, I have long asserted that the real hope of reducing charges upon our bulk goods was through the modernization of our great interior waterways. By modernization, I mean increasing depths to a point where we can handle ten thousand tons in a line of barges pulled by a tug. This administration has authorized the systematic undertaking of this modernization. Within a few years we will have completed the deepening of the Ohio up to Pittsburgh, the Missouri up to Kansas City, Omaha, and beyond, the Mississippi to St. Paul and Minneapolis, the Illinois to Chicago. We already have experience with results, for with only the main river from St. Louis to New Orleans as yet working properly the rates for transportation of bulk agricultural products through that section are near pre-war railway rates. We will not have the advantage of full results until the entire Mississippi and its tributaries are in one connected transportation system.

The St. Lawrence Project

We have another great opportunity of relief in the

building of a shipway from the Great Lakes to the sea. Our engineers have recommended the St. Lawrence route as the preferable outlet. The administration has undertaken negotiations with Canada upon the subject. If these negotiations fail, we must consider alternative routes. In any event, the completion of this great system of barge lines on the rivers and connecting the lakes with the Gulf, of opening a shipway from the lakes to the sea, will make an effective transportation system 12,000 miles in length penetrating twenty Midwest states. It will connect these states with seaboard at the Gulf on one hand and with the North Atlantic on the other. And this means more than the mere saving upon the actual goods shipped over these routes. If part of our crops can move to market at a seven- to ten-cent saving per bushel, the buyers' competitive bidding for this portion of the crop will force upward the price of the whole crop.

And this development concerns not alone agriculture, but every industry and business in the Midwest. The manufacturer and merchant in this section is suffering from a curtailment of his distribution field; his business province has shrunk. This development should tend to increase manufacturing industry in the Midwest and thereby create a larger diversity of employment and a greater local market for agricultural products. Nor does this development mean the crippling of our railways. The annual increase in railway traffic will give to them a far more than complete offset to these diversions. Moreover, everything that increases the prosperity of the country also helps the railways. The policy of rapid consummation of this great project will be continued if the Republican administration be continued. We should at the present rate of progress have completed the Mississippi system within the next four years. It is a vital part of the rehabilitation of the Middle West agriculture and business.

Enduring Nature of American Integrity

The modernizations of our waterways recall again the earlier life of Iowa. At one time its transportation was in large degree over these same rivers, and many of our pioneers reached this state by the old packet boats and their own rafts. Nor are the days of the pioneer over. We have to pioneer through economic problems, through scientific development and invention, on to frontiers just as forbidding, just as romantic, and just as pregnant of added happiness as our fathers ever knew. The test of our generation will be whether we can overcome these frontiers, whether we can hold mastery over the system we have created, whether we can maintain the advantage we have inherited, whether we can hold ourselves a nation dedicated to equal opportunity for all.

There are those in this audience who saw Iowa an open prairie. I recall members of my own family who in my childhood were still breaking the soil in the western part of the state and were then still living in the first sod houses of the pioneer farmer. Our fathers and grandfathers who poured over the Midwest were self-reliant, rugged, God-fearing people of indomitable courage. They combined to build the roads, bridges, and towns; they co-operated together to erect their schools, their churches, and to raise their barns and harvest their fields. They asked only for freedom of opportunity and an equal chance. In these conceptions lies the real basis of American democracy. They and their fathers gave a genius to American institutions that distinguished our people from any other in the world. Their demand for an equal chance is the basis of American progress. To those who have by necessity worked in other lands comes this most vivid meaning of America and a deep gratitude for what our fathers have builded. Here there are no limits to hope, no limits upon accomplishment; our obligation today is to maintain that equal opportunity for agriculture as well as for every other calling.

When we traverse the memories of those who have builded this state and this nation we recall these acts which are rooted in the soil of service. When we rehearse our own memories we find that none give us such comfort and satisfaction as the record of service we have been able to render. I do not believe our people have lost those finer qualities of rugged character, self-reliance, or initiative, nor have they lost the great quality which they embedded in American character, the quality of neighborly co-operation and mutual service. It is in this quality that our hopes must lie in the solution of our great problems.

End and Aim of Government

And I must say again that the solution of these problems has but one purpose—that is, the comfort and welfare of the American family and the American home. The family is the unit of American life and the home is the sanctuary of moral inspiration and of American spirit. The true conception of America is not a country of 110,000,000 people but a nation of 23,000,000 families living in 23,000,000 homes. I pledge my services to these homes.

After an all-day automobile tour through Essex County, including a visit to the laboratories of Thomas A. Edison, Mr. Hoover spoke at the State Armory in Newark.

NEWARK, NEW JERSEY

September 17, 1928

Real wages and standards of living of our labor have improved more during the past seven and one-half years of Republican rule than during any similar period in the history of this or of any other country.

When I speak of wages I refer both to those who work at the bench and those who work at the desk. Nor is this addressed to men alone. More than ten million women march to work every morning side by side with the men. Steadily the importance of women is gaining not only in the routine tasks of industry but in executive responsibility. I include also the woman who stays at home as the guardian of the welfare of the family. She is a partner in the job and the wages. Women constitute a part of our industrial achievement.

Stable Employment Fundamental

I wish to lay down the proposition that the very prerequisite, the very foundation, of economic progress to our industrial and business employees is full and stable employment. A continued surplus of unemployed workers means decreasing wages, increasing hours, and fear for the future. To protect labor, to maintain its prosperity, to abolish poverty, we must so organize our economic system as to provide a job for all who have the will to work.

Full employment depends not only upon a strong and progressive economic system but upon the sound policies of and the vigorous co-operation by the government to promote economic welfare. Labor in its collective efforts has contributed greatly to the maintenance of proper wages and to improved conditions of labor. But collective bargaining cannot overcome the forces that make for unemployment. I, for one, am willing to trust the proved ability of employees to take care of their rights if there is employment to be had. And our workers as citizens at the ballot box have a large part in the determination of these economic policies.

The problem of insuring full work all the time is a problem of national concern. It is one to which government must give its attention. It is one which government may contribute to solve. Behind every job is a vast, intricate, and delicately adjusted system of interlocked industries dependent upon skilled leadership and upon finding a market for their products at home or in foreign lands. The forces of credit, communications, transportation, power, foreign relations, and what not must all be kept in tune if steady employment is to be assured. A failure in any part imposes a penalty upon labor through unemployment. Break this chain of relationship at any point and the whole machine is thrown out of order. Close down a New Jersey factory because of inadequate transportation or inadequate tariff and its effect is felt by the New Jersey truck farmer. Cease exporting automobiles to South America or Europe, and automobile workers are thrown out of employment in Michigan. The suffering does not stop there. It only begins. The steel mills slacken in Pennsylvania and Indiana. The mines employ fewer workers at Lake Superior. And every farmer in the United States suffers from the diminished purchasing power and enforced stringency in thousands of homes.

Achievements of Present Administration

The modern relationships of government and industry are a tangled mass of economic and social problems. They are neither abstract propositions nor statistics. They are very human beings. They can make for the happiness of every home in our country.

The Republican Party has performed unparalleled service to the employees in our commerce and industry throughout its history and notably during the past seven and one-half years. Continuous employment and prosperity of labor depend upon the continuance of those policies. It is these wider issues of governmental responsibility in laying broad and deep foundations of employment that I wish to discuss tonight. The Republican Party recognizes this responsibility. Proof of this rests upon its actual record of accomplishment. That record can be tested by examination of the situation of labor in the country today.

When we assumed direction of the government in 1921 there were five to six millions unemployed upon our streets. Wages and salaries were falling and hours of labor increasing. Anxiety for daily bread haunted nearly one-quarter of our 23,000,000 families.

The Republican administration at once undertook to find relief for this situation. At once a nation-wide employment conference was called. It was made up of representatives of both employers and employees. I had the honor to be chairman of that conference. We set up a program for the systematic organization of the whole business community to restore employment. By means of immediate institution of public works, the extension of financial aid to industry during the critical period of readjustment, by co-operation of employers, and by a score of other devices, we started the wheels of industry turning again. We did not resort to the expedients of some foreign countries, of doles, subsidies, charity, or inflation—all of which in the end are borne by the people.

Within a year we restored these five million workers

66

to employment. But we did more, we produced a fundamental program which made this restored employment secure on foundations of prosperity. As a result wages and standards of living have during the past six and one-half years risen to steadily higher levels. This recovery and this stability are no accident. It has not been achieved by luck. Were it not for sound governmental policies and wise leadership, employment conditions in America today would be similar to those existing in many other parts of the world. None of the larger countries engaged in the Great War have as yet restored full employment. Doles to the idle and other devices of desperation still exist abroad.

Current Unemployment Diminishing

There have been assertions of wide unemployment at the present time. There was a temporary dip of employment last winter. From this we are now rapidly recovering. Its causes were local and temporary. They were the combined effect of the Mississippi flood, a great shift in the motor industry, and the collapse of real estate speculation. An accurate survey of the Department of Labor showed that, even including the usual winter seasonal unemployment, about 1,800,000 employees were out of work as contrasted with five to six millions in 1921. During the past two months there has been a higher record of production and consumption of goods than during corresponding months of any previous year. There could not be such a record unless employment was steadily recovering.

There are two industries which have only partially recovered to our general industrial prosperity. They are the bituminous coal and the textile industries. Here the difficulties of recovery from overexpansion during the war have been increased by a duplication of part of both industries in the Southern states. They have also been affected by changes in use of textiles on one hand and by the increase of electricity on the other. We have a duty to continue effort to their full recovery by every assistance that the government can afford. This will be carried forward diligently.

Prevalent High Wages

Despite these rare exceptions, the average of real wages is higher today than ever before. And the arduous hours of labor have decreased. We can easily prove this. As a standard of comparison let us take the purchasing power of wages in 1913 or before the war. In purchasing power we consider both the dollars paid and the cost of living. Taking this standard we shall find that real wages at the height of the war inflation were about thirty per cent over 1913. Despite the great after-war slump they have risen until today they are over fifty per cent greater than before the war. Viewed in another way, while the cost of living today is about sixty points on the index above pre-war, wages are one hundred and twenty-seven above. Parallel with this increase in real wages the average hours of labor have steadily decreased.

Moreover our real wages and our standards of living are the highest in the world. And I am again speaking of the real buying power of wages. To compare ours with foreign wages we must find a common denominator, because translation of foreign currencies means but little. If we say that five per cent of butter and ninety-five per cent of flour form the basis of that useful mixture called "bread and butter," then the weekly earnings in each country would buy at retail in those countries the following total of this useful compound. Please note these figures carefully.

WEEKLY WAGES IF APPLIED TO THE PURCHASE OF "COMPOSITE POUNDS OF BREAD AND BUTTER"

(Each pound 95 per cent wheat flour and 5 per cent butter)

	Railway Engineers	Carpenters	Electricians	Coal Miners	Weavers	Day Labor
United States	717	731	778	558	323	259
United Kingdom	367	262	267	267	136	160
Germany	217	173	158	133	106	112
France	269	94	123	136	73	68
Belgium	150	96	76	94	94	65
Italy	166	151	152	95	75	110
Sweden	261	256	224	180	155	162
Japan	164	125	96	60	83	66

Of course the American employee does not use his higher income to buy unnecessary pounds of bread and butter. He uses it to diversify and expand his consumption of all things. It spells better homes, automobiles, radios, and a thousand things for the family that were utterly unknown a generation ago, and are still utterly unknown to the average citizen in most countries of the world. Fear of poverty has been reduced. Fear of loss of employment has been lessened by stability. Fear of old age and for the future of the family has been lessened through increased payments to the savings banks, to the insurance companies, and to our labor benefit societies.

The Government's Share Extensive

Before I discuss the policies by which this has been brought about let me say that the Republican administration makes no claim to credit which belongs to the enterprise, energy, and character of a great people. Education, prohibition, invention, scientific discovery, increase in skill in managers and employees have contributed to magnificent progress. But all of these efforts would be incomplete and the margin of employment would have been less had it not been for the co-operative actions taken by the government. And it is this margin of employment which makes for the safety or the danger of labor.

Protection

The first of our policies which have given security and expansion of employment has been the enactment of the protective tariff. The protective tariff has been a fundamental policy of the Republican Party ever since the party was founded. Against it the Democratic Party has battled for these same seventy years. Two months ago their platform hinted that they thought we might be right. However, they declared for a tariff that would maintain effective competition. That must mean a tariff which will maintain effective competition of foreign against American goods. That is not protection. That this is the meaning is borne out by references to the Underwood Tariff of the last Democratic administration as the ideal. The re-enactment of that tariff would let in a flood of foreign goods, destroy employment and lower wages, and demoralize our farmers all over the United States. I would suggest that the employees of industries in New Jersey and the country should directly investigate as to what would happen to their employment with lowered tariffs.

Immigration

The Republican administration imposed restrictions upon immigration largely to protect the American workman. With the bars of immigration down the flow of those seeking relief from the poverty of Europe would create a horde of job hunters around every employment office and every industrial gate in the United States. The pressure of this flood would break our wages toward the levels of Europe.

No one places a higher worth upon the foreign-born citizen than I do. He brings many elements of great value in our cultural development. We welcome his help in building our new civilization. The immigration laws should be amended to remedy the hardships to families. I have urged before that this be done. In my acceptance speech I stated my opposition to any increase in immigration. The restriction upon immigration is a boon not only to those of my hearers who were born on American soil but to those who have come from the old countries, for every one would suffer equally by the lowering of our wages and standards of living.

The enactment of this law was opposed on economic grounds. I do not here propose to enter into the arguments which were advanced in perfect good faith that production in America would shrink because we would have too few workers, that the cost of living would thus increase, or that it would destroy America's ability to compete in the shipment of her goods into foreign markets. I did not agree with those arguments. I believe that the maintenance of the higher standards of living stimulates the development of labor-saving devices, increases skill in our workmen and in our managers, and that in this way we compensate for higher wages. It is proving itself so today. We are exporting more goods abroad than ever in our history. We are gradually lowering the cost of living by greater efficiency.

There is no measure on our statute books today that represents a more fundamental, sound, and important step in true progress than does this new charter of American labor. It is the necessary and natural companion piece of a protective tariff. In the one instance we protect the American worker from the goods of foreign factories, made under their lower standards of living. In the other case, we check the excess labor flooding through our doors to reduce the American wage.

Foreign Trade

When at the beginning of the Republican administration we were determining those measures which would restore and increase employment, one of our first decisions was vigorously to build up our foreign trade. We determined that we must sell more products abroad if we would have steady and assured employment for labor in our industries. We realized that we must energetically promote the sale of our farmers' surplus abroad both in their interest and in the interest of labor. By so doing we increase the farmer's buying power and in turn his demand for the products of labor.

When we came into office we were confronted with a total disorganization of the world trade due to the war. We had been exporting great quantities of munitions. This business was finished. World trade was demoralized to such an extent that the actual movement of

73

commodities between all nations was some twenty per cent less than before the war.

We set out upon a definitely organized campaign to build up the export of the products of American labor and of the American farm. We reorganized the Department of Commerce for the promotion of American trade abroad on a greater scale than had ever been achieved or ever attempted by any government anywhere in the world. We mobilized our manufacturers and exporters; co-operated with them in laying out and executing strategic plans to expand our foreign trade in all directions. That this great part played by the government is no hypothetical assertion is amply evidenced by the fact that the daily applications for assistance by exporters to the Department have steadily increased from five hundred daily in 1922 to an average of ten thousand a day in 1928. In the last year before the war our total exports were a little under $2,500,000,000. In 1922, the first year of the Republican administration, they were $3,750,000,000. The dollar since the war has not been as valuable a dollar as in 1913. If we make a correction so as to estimate them on a quantity basis, we find that our exports for 1922 were, in pre-war dollars, about $2,730,000,000. During the year 1927 our exports were $4,750,000,000, and if for comparison we convert this figure to the pre-war value of the dollar they were $3,840,000,000. Thus on any calculation our exports have increased by over one billion dollars during the past seven years. This is an increase of forty-one per cent since 1922 and an increase of fifty-eight per cent over pre-war.

Recent Growth No Accident

Now, I want to clearly show what this means. It was not due to world recovery. If we make a survey of the world's trade today, we shall find that the export trade of all countries is only ten per cent above pre-war, while ours is fifty-eight per cent. Also, if we make a survey of what has happened to the other great trading nations who were engaged in the war, we find that their foreign trade for the year 1927, when it is similarly adjusted for the depreciation of money, shows only a bare recovery to pre-war bases. It is no accident which has brought about this unique situation in the United States. It is not chance that has brought this added employment for American workmen, and added markets for American farmers. Things like that don't happen.

More than two million families in the United States earn their living today producing goods for export, and another million families earn their living in the manufacture of raw materials which we import in exchange for our exports. This increase in exports has brought a living to a half-million families. This means more than statistics. It means higher standards of living—more jobs make more wages. Foreign trade is no artificial stimulant to employment. Its development is a vital contribution to the welfare of the American workman and the American merchant and the American farmer. I propose that we shall continue this service to our people.

Unity of Labor and Other Interests

One of the large opportunities for the further improvement of labor lies in the further improvement of agriculture. Some of its most important branches have lagged behind industry in its advance since the war. This is not an occasion to enter upon that question, but by sympathetic policies we should materially further increase the farmers' buying power and thus add to the security of employment in the industries. This becomes one of our first duties in common interest.

American labor has been the first labor body in the world that has had the intelligence and courage to realize and express the fact that increased wages and salaries must in the long run be based upon a sharing of labor in the savings made through industrial and commercial efficiency. Within the past few months British labor has followed this lead of American labor. That is, if we are able by labor-saving machinery and reduction of the wastes in industry to decrease the cost of production of an article, we know by long experience that a train of consequences of the highest importance follow. Wages in that industry will rise, prices decrease, consumption increase at home and in our foreign markets, the demand for labor is enlarged, and our standards of living improve. The ancient bitter opposition to improved methods on the ancient theory that it more than temporarily deprives men of employment, which is still maintained in some parts of the world, has no place in the gospel of American progress.

The Elimination of Waste

Eight years ago I caused a nation-wide investigation to be undertaken of the whole subject. I felt that it was in the interest of our country to know what opportunities we had to improve our methods. It developed that there were great opportunities for increased efficiency in our whole industrial machine. We have the highest ingenuity and efficiency, in the operation of our individual industries, of any nation. Yet there were great wastes which were not the fault of individuals, employers, or employees. These wastes were due to seasonal unemployment and to unemployment during depressions; to speculation and overproduction during booms; to labor turnover and labor conflicts; to intermittent failure of transportation, of supplies, of fuel, of power, and of credit to synchronize with demand; to lack of simplification and standardization in many of our commonly used commodities; to losses in our processes and materials and scores of other directions. They all combined

77

to represent a huge deduction from the goods and services and employment we might all enjoy if we could but eliminate these wastes.

We adopted a new policy in government. That was, that the Secretary of Commerce should co-operate with industry in organization against such waste, not by law or regulation, but by purely voluntary action in which the joint service of the associations representing the managers of a given industry, its employees, its distributors, and its consumers were all enlisted in a common purpose. We have had magnificent co-operation from the leaders and the employees of American business. I will not take your time to recite the literally thousands of co-operative actions undertaken and carried through with beneficent results, but I will give an illustration.

From time immemorial the building industry has been a seasonal business. It was idle a large part of the winter. The first conference upon reducing its seasonal character was called under my chairmanship in 1923. It was participated in by manufacturers of building material, by contractors, by engineers, by real estate men, by representatives of the employees. An exhaustive examination by this body resulted in the conclusion that the average seasonal unemployment in the building trades was about one hundred days out of the year. A number of specific remedies were initiated by organized co-operation in different centers. By this co-operative action and by improved methods the average days of unemployment have been decreased by nearly one-half.

There has been no decrease in daily wages. In fact, there has been increase in wages; but far more important, the annual income of workers in the building trades has been substantially increased by the decrease in idle days. It has enabled us to increase the total annual volume of building with the same complement of labor and equipment. It has decreased the unit cost of building and contributed to the expansion of building generally. Nor are the benefits confined to the construction industries. They give greater stability to all the manufacturers of building material and to transportation.

Diminishing Industrial Irregularity

As another instance of an action of fundamental importance to labor I might mention the organization of measures in the government to mitigate the violence of the so-called business cycle. That is, the recurrent periods of boom and false hope, waste and extravagance, followed by hard times with their hideous unemployment, decreasing wages, bankruptcy in business, and ruinous prices to the farmer. These booms and slumps have occurred periodically for seventy-five years, although less than half as often under Republican as under Democratic administrations. The great unemployment period of 1921 was the direct result of war inflation and the boom of 1920. No one has suffered more from these movements than our salary and wage earners.

Time forbids a discussion of the intricate problems involved or the remedies which we have inaugurated. They include better organization of credit, advance information as to demand for industrial products, as to volume of their production, as to the use of public construction in slack times, and many other methods. As a result of co-operation with industry and banking and public officials, we have greatly mitigated this most dangerous of all disasters to our breadwinners. The proof lies in the fact that we have had a far longer period of stability in industry and commerce and in the far greater security of employment than ever before in our history.

In my speech of acceptance I outlined our national programs of prospective public works, including the development of water resources, public roads, and the construction of public buildings. In that speech I pointed out that these projects would require upwards of one billion dollars within the next four years. I there recommended that, so far as practicable, this work should be carried on in such a way as to take up the slack of occasional unemployment.

While the judicious arrangement of government construction work can aid in wiping out the unemployment caused by seasonal variations in business activity, the Federal Government can do more. The Department of

Labor should be authorized to undertake the collection of regular statistics upon seasonal and other unemployment. We must have this fundamental information for further attack upon this problem, from the further solution of which will come still greater stability and prosperity in the world of employer and employee.

Increase in Efficiency

We have gained enormously in efficiency in our whole economic machinery in the past seven years. I cannot take the time to recite to you the extraordinary evidence of this. I hesitate to express it statistically lest I appear to exaggerate. Taken as a whole we have swelled our production on a quantity basis by nearly thirty per cent. Parallel with it wages have risen and the prices of manufactured goods have fallen.

I have heard voices raised in protest that the effect of these activities is to destroy employment. This is a re-echo of a century ago. As a matter of fact we have gone through an extraordinary industrial revolution in seven years and we do not find any such unemployment as would be implied by these protests. There are individual cases of unemployment in these shifts, but wise policies and co-operation with industry have rendered them but momentary. The reasons why no dangers lie in store are simple enough.

As we transfer the burden from the backs of men to

machines we increase the wages of workers. We increase their buying power. We create a demand for new commodities and new services. By the energies and capital which we have released through increased efficiency of the older industries we have been able to expand other industries and to create new ones to further employment, and to supply new additions to the comfort of every home.

From these and other causes we see a great expansion in the automobile industry, in telephones and electric lights. In seven years we have seen the radio industry emerge from a few hundred thousands to hundreds of millions in its product. We have seen the aeroplane industry develop from almost nothing seven years ago to a most potent industry today. Due to increased efficiency hundreds of thousands of men and women have been transferred from the factories to our expanding insurance and banking to take care of enlarged savings; other hundreds of thousands have been transferred to our filling stations, our garages, our hotels, and our restaurants. We have in this period seen a half-million families find occupation in increased export of goods, and, above all, we have seen an increase of nearly two million youths taken largely from the potential ranks of labor and placed in institutions of education. This is proof of real progress. It is the road to further progress. It is the road to abolition of poverty.

Improved Industrial Relations

I have already stated the position of the Republican Party in positive support of free collective bargaining. I have stated that it is necessary to impose restrictions on the excessive use of injunctions. It is my desire and the desire of every good citizen to ameliorate the causes of industrial conflict, to build toward that true co-operation which must be the foundation of common action for the common welfare. The first requisite to less conflict is full employment. By full employment we are steadily reducing conflict and loss.

The whole relationship between employer and employee has shown great improvement in these past seven years. During these years there has been a revolution through shifting of basic ideas on the part of both business and labor. The large majority of both sides today willingly accept the fundamental principle that the highest possible wages are the road to increased consumption of goods and thereby to prosperity. Both accept the fundamental fact that greater efficiency, larger application of mechanical devices, and full personal effort are the road to cheaper costs, lower prices, and thus again to wider consumption and larger production of goods. Both discard the ancient contention that labor is an economic commodity. Both realize that labor is entitled to participation in the benefits of increased efficiency by increased wage, either directly or through the decrease in living

83

costs. Both have joined in repelling socialism and other subversive movements.

He would be a rash man who would state that we are finally entering the industrial millennium, but there is a great ray of hope that America is finding herself on the road to a solution of the greatest of all her problems. That problem is to adjust our economic system to our social ideals. We are making progress toward social peace and contentment with the preservation of private industry, of initiative, and full development of the individual. Working out of this ideal cannot be attained by compulsory settlement of employee and employer conflicts by the hand of the government. It cannot be attained by placing the government in business and reducing our people to bureaucracies.

It is idle to argue that there are no longer any conflicts of interest between employee and employer. But there are wide areas of activity in which their interests should coincide, and it is the part of statesmanship to organize and increase this identity of interest in order to limit the area of conflict. Conflict diminishes and common purpose flourishes only in prosperity and in an encouraging atmosphere of sound governmental policies.

Change in National Policies Unwise

At such a time as this a change in national policies involves not only a choice between different roads by either of which we may go forward — as some may lightly think—but a question also as to whether we may not be taking the wrong road and moving backward. The measure of our national prosperity, of our stability, of our hope of further progress at this time, is the measure of what we may risk through a change in present policies. More than once in our national history a change in policies in a time of advancement has been quickly followed by a turn toward disaster.

Our economic system has abuses; it has grave faults in its operation. But we can build toward perfection only upon a foundation of prosperity. Poverty is not the cause of progress. Enduring national life cannot be builded upon the bowed and sweating backs of oppressed and embittered men and women. It must be uplifted and up-held by the willing and eager hands of the whole people. They will uphold it if our economic life be built for the whole people, not for any special group.

Sources of Leadership

To assure this sort of progress our first necessity is to assure the ability and character of our leadership. It requires that we secure into its ranks all of the intelligence and character of our race—that it be sympathetic with the life and aims of all of our 23,000,000 homes. At no time have we had more able leaders in economic life than today. At no time have we been more certain that the fiber and intelligence of our people furnishes a vast reservoir of such leadership adequate to the future. But able administrators, skilled workers, professional and moral leaders cannot be made by birth or money. They cannot be selected by divine right or through bureaucracy. Nor can their ranks be filled from a limited class.

Our leadership can be found and it will be sympathetic to our ideals if we maintain the decency and dignity of family life through a stable economic system; if we maintain free and universal education and thus provide them the open stair to leadership; if we maintain for every individual an equality of opportunity to attain that position in the community to which his character and his ability entitle him. Then our supply of leadership will stream forward of its own impulse. It is in this insistence upon an equal chance and a free road to rise in leadership that our great American experiment has departed from those of history. It is our sure guarantee of the future. In its vast possibilities is the hope of every mother for her boys and her girls.

Under such leadership, replenished constantly from the great mass of our people, we can aspire to a democracy which will express a common purpose for the common good. We can build a civilization where national conscience is alert to protect the rights of all, curtail selfish economic power, and hold to the ideal of distributed contentment among the whole people.

Mr. Hoover spoke in the Harmon Field amphitheater at Elizabethton on the occasion of the celebration of the one hundred and forty-eighth anniversary of the Battle of Kings Mountain in the War for Independence. The speaker's stand faced a rolling meadow, rising to a tree-covered mountain. Mr. Hoover was introduced by Alfred A. Taylor, Republican, former governor of Tennessee, and brother of the no less famous "Fiddlin' Bob" Taylor, Democrat, also at one time governor of the state.

ELIZABETHTON, TENNESSEE

October 6, 1928

I AM proud to have been invited as your guest in this celebration of your progress and this review of your part in national history.

When Southerners go North or Northerners go South to deliver public addresses they seem to feel it necessary to first launch into an explanation that all lines of sectionalism have disappeared in the United States. I am from the West, where our people are proud to be the melted product of both the North and the South. Our accent differs from that of the people of Alabama and Vermont, but we have the same hearts, the same kind of homes, the same ideals and aspirations. Every morning and evening we read the same news; every night we listen by radio to the same voices. Our mental and physical frontiers are gone. It happens that we need geographical divisions for statistical and descriptive use, but otherwise we could leave this question to orators and humorists.

Your celebration today raises many memories of our national beginnings. Patriotism is of many inspirations.

It receives refreshment from many springs. None are more powerful than our traditions of service, of suffering, of accomplishment, and of heroism. The rivulets of these traditions from every part of our country in the course of history merge into that great stream of national memories which is the constant refreshment of national ideals. These memories are indeed the imponderable force which builds and cements our national life.

Greatness of Southern Pioneers

To the Westerner, appreciative of history and tradition, this occasion presents a double significance. As you have shown today, this locality was once the nation's frontier. Here were enacted some of the most stirring scenes in the brilliant drama of our pioneer era. Seven years before the Declaration of Independence there came to the banks of the Watauga—which was then the Far West—the first permanent settlers. They were soon followed by others from the back country of North Carolina. In these settlements, frontiersmen remote from the centers of civilization, freed by difficult distance from the sway of all governmental authority, voluntarily created their own frame of popular government. They erected what was to all practical purposes a free and independent state, under their own constitution.

In the Articles of the Watauga Association were implanted some of the great principles which later found permanent lodgment in our fundamental law. Similar associations sprang into being in other parts of these mountains. Historians of our frontier agree that no more striking proof of the native capacity of our early Americans for local self-government was ever given than by these associations. They not only created a government. The Watauga men, determined in their independence, rallied to the improvised army during the Revolution which at Kings Mountain struck a decisive blow for the colonial cause.

They with their compatriots from Virginia and the Carolinas attacked and disastrously defeated a formidable army under competent leadership, fading again into the forest as soon as their task was accomplished. No battle more dramatic or marked by courage and skill of a higher order has been fought on this continent. It was a turning-point in the Revolutionary War. It compelled the retirement of General Cornwallis toward the coast, revived the flagging spirit of the discouraged colonists, and opened the way for the final victory at Yorktown. I wish to compliment you upon your pageant commemorating these achievements.

Their Influence in the West

These states in common with those to the north began the greatest drama of all history—the spread of Americans from a feeble foothold on the Atlantic seaboard to the most powerful nation in the world in scarce two centuries. The great West was won not by the action of the government, but by the individual effort of intrepid and courageous men from all these Atlantic states. They builded their own self-government. Tennessee, Kentucky, and Texas were gained by pioneers under Sevier, Robertson, Clark, Boone, Houston, and others. They won not only homes for themselves, but for a long time determined the course of history westward. The Mississippi River ceased to be a boundary, and year after year the powerful pulsation of westward expansion throbbed with heroism and sacrifice. They were ready to fight for the simple right of self-government. General Fremont, the pathfinder to the Pacific Coast, came from Georgia, and true to tradition he fought for and erected the first self-government of my own state of California.

To me it is an inspiration to be standing on this spot, for in a sense I have a common heritage with you. The earliest ancestor of whom I have record, Andrew Hoover, a settler in Maryland about two centuries ago, migrated to North Carolina and built his home a hundred miles from this spot. In Randolph County of that state he did his part in building the community, and his grave lies in the little burying-ground on what was then the Uharrie River farm. His son, my great-great-grandfather, was part of that movement which started west from your frontier.

As Secretary of Commerce I have been profoundly interested in the amazing progress of the South in this past seven and one-half years. In order that the Department might assist to the fullest extent in that progress, we increased our branch offices in the South from three in 1920 to twenty-nine in 1928. As a result of the contact thus established we were able to observe your increasing prosperity.

The record is impressive. There are in the South about 8,000,000 families, and in this period they have shown increase in numbers by perhaps ten per cent. Contrasted with this, the manufacturing output has increased by over sixty per cent. The number of employees has increased by over thirty per cent. The value of crops has increased by over forty-five per cent. The shipments from Southern ports have increased by fifty per cent; the net income of your railways has grown by over one hundred and forty per cent; electrical power in use has been increased by one hundred and twenty-five per cent. The postal receipts have grown by forty-five per cent. That this enormous increase in wealth and production has had wide distribution can be seen on every hand. It is indicated by increased wages and decreased cost of living; in twenty per cent of new homes, in a gain of one hundred and fifty per cent of automobiles and thirty per cent in telephones. Life insurance in force has increased by seventy per cent and bank clearings have increased by fifty per cent. Depositors in savings banks have more than doubled. Building and loan association assets have increased one hundred and eighty per cent. In nearly every case these percentages exceed the corresponding increase in the country as a whole. All this has been accomplished in seven and one-half years.

In every phase of life the South is moving forward. New vistas of betterment are opening. The ability and energy of the people is constantly growing and is of more dynamic scope. They have engaged in every form of useful community effort to improve both the material and spiritual side of life.

I have had the honor to be president of the Better-Homes Association. In that organization over two thousand towns have actively co-operated throughout the South during this past year. Fourteen out of twenty-four of the annual prizes given by this association for the most successful work during the last five years have been awarded to the Southern committees for leadership in bettering homes. Moreover, as director in various national committees devoted to increase of playgrounds and public parks, I have had occasion to note with gratification the extraordinary progress made throughout the South in the provision for wholesome recreation. You have not been negligent of education. In the past seven years the attendance in high schools has increased by ninety-one per cent and in institutions of higher learning by seventy per cent. Your moral and spiritual foundations have been strengthened.

I know that the people of the South will agree with me that these results could never have been attained but for helpful co-operation and sound policies in the national government, and that change of these policies can bring only distress and disaster.

Local Leadership Responsible

The South possesses vast resources of raw materials and electrical power, easy access to the sea, a great reserve of labor, a wealth of soil, a moderate climate. Most of these factors have been here always. Such resources exist in many other countries, but if they are not accompanied by fine leadership, by intellect and character as well as sound policies of government, there could be no such development as we have witnessed in the South during this last seven years. That leadership has not been by immigration from the North. It has been the product of Southern men and women. The South has again proved to have in her blood that strain of leadership and fortitude which contributed so much to found our republic and so much to build our own West.

His Candidacy Truly National

I realize that I come here as the candidate of a political party with whose policies many of you within my sight and many within the sound of my voice have often differed. I respect your views regarding that difference. Yet so closely welded in common interest are the pressing issues of our nation today that it should be no longer unusual for a citizen of any region to vote for a president who represents the principles which correspond with his convictions.

Our national officials are chosen in order that they may protect the political and economic health of the American people. In a contest such as this there is no place for personal bitterness. A great attribute of our political life has been the spirit of fair play with which our presidential contests have been waged in former years and the sportsmanlike spirit in which we have accepted the result. We prove ourselves worthy of self-government and worthy of confidence as officials in proportion as we keep these contests free from abuse, free from misrepresentation, and free from words and acts which carry regret. Whatever the result, we remain fellow-countrymen.

No better illustration of true sportsmanship in American politics can be found than in the historic contest waged in this state between two brilliant brothers, one of whom honors us with his presence at this meeting, the beloved Alfred Taylor of Tennessee. In the annals of chivalry no chapter portrays human nature to better advantage than your own "War of the Roses" in which Alfred Taylor, the Republican, and Robert Taylor, the

Democrat, engaged in fierce political combat, attracted the attention of the whole nation, and stirred this whole state from center to circumference. Yet in the heat of strife they kept in mind the advice of that good mother who had admonished her two stalwart sons never to forget the tie of brotherhood. It is in that spirit I wish to discuss the problems that concern our country and the methods I believe necessary to obtain their solution.

Post-War Changes in Our Civilization

Our country has entered upon an entirely new era. For fourteen years our attention in public life has been mainly given to the Great War and reconstruction from it. These fourteen years have witnessed a revolution in our world relations, in many phases of our economic life and our relations of government to them. Due to the ingenuity and hard work of our people and the sound policies in government, we have come since the war to be the greatest reservoir of the world's wealth. We have transformed ourselves from a country borrowing capital from abroad to the foremost lender of capital to foreign countries. Our people, growing in efficiency and productive power, are pressing for expansion of world markets. Competition for these markets grows keener each year. Our increasing foreign trade has penetrated into every country in the world. Political diseases arising from the war misery of foreign countries have at times disturbed us by their infection of certain of our people. The poverty of Europe presses huge immigration toward us. We still have unsettled debts due us from the war. For all these reasons our international relations have vastly increased. By our growth of wealth and power we have a great burden of responsibility for the peace of the world. Abolition of the liquor traffic has become a part of our fundamental law and great problems of enforcement and obedience to law have arisen from it. From the violence of the war we have inherited increase in crime. Technicalities of court procedure have been used to defeat justice and to aid law violators. The invention of the gas engine has brought the automobile and the aeroplane. It has shortened distances, but it has brought new problems in roads and traffic.

Discoveries in electricity have meant an immense expansion in power and communication, which bring also their problems of regulation to protect public rights. The war has vastly increased the expenditures of the government. The assessment of taxes and expenditures of public monies have come to bear a vital part in business stability. During these years we have adopted a measure of federal control of credit. Errors in that delicate adjustment can cause us fabulous losses. The war has dislocated our transportation relations both within our country and with foreign countries. Development of inland waterways, of merchant marine, and consolidation of railways are forced upon us. More acute than all are the readjustments in the world's producing and consuming power. Great expansion of agricultural production in Canada and the Southern Hemisphere, combined with increasing efficiency and larger production by our own farmers, has rendered unstable those branches of our agriculture which are dependent upon foreign markets. These circumstances have brought a long train of difficulties to the American farmer. With fewer men needed upon the farm and with more needed in other lines of production, our great cities have, within this fourteen years, a little less than doubled in population, with resultant social problems. Increasing skill and prosperity have brought us more material comfort and greater leisure but also serious questions as to how we should use our leisure time. New inventions, including the automobile and the radio, have brought us into closer relations with our neighbors, and given us a keener knowledge of each other, a broader vision of the world, and higher ambitions. This higher standard of living, this new prosperity, is dependent upon an economic system vastly more intricate and delicately adjusted than ever before. It now must be kept in perfect tune if we would not, through its dislocation, have a breakdown in employment and in the standards of living of our people. From all this, new moral and spiritual as well as economic problems crowd upon us.

Consequent Function of Government

Our government was created in the belief that economic activities—that is, the forces of business and commerce—would translate themselves into widely distributed public welfare if left alone by the government. The government has come more and more to touch this delicate web at a thousand points. We indeed wish the government to leave it alone to the utmost degree, but yearly the relations of government to national prosperity become more and more intimate regardless of what we wish to think. All this places a greater strain upon the flexibility of our government and should give us deep concern over every extension of its authority lest we overburden it to the breaking-point.

I wish to remind you of something which may sound humble and commonplace, but it vibrates through every hope of the future. It is this—the unit of American life is the family and the home. It is the economic unit as well as the moral and spiritual unit. But it is more than this. It is the beginning of self-government. It is the throne of our highest ideals. It is the source of the spiritual energy of our people. For the perfecting of this unit of national life we must bend all of our material and scientific ingenuity. For the attainment of this end we must lend every energy of the government.

I have before emphasized that the test of our government is what it does to insure that the home is secure in material benefit and comfort; what it does to keep that home free from bureaucratic domination; what it does to open the door of opportunity to every boy and girl within it; what it does in building moral safeguards and strengthening moral and spiritual inspiration. From the homes of America must emanate that purity of inspiration only as a result of which we can succeed in self-government. I speak of this as a basic principle that should guide our national life. I speak of it as the living action of government in the building of a nation. I speak of it as the source from which government must rise to higher and higher standards of perfection from year to year.

I cannot within the limits of time discuss in detail the policies of our government or the solution of the multitude of issues that confront us and the attitude of my party and myself toward them. I shall mention shortly those which have more particular interest to the South. As never before does the keeping of our economic machine in tune depend upon wise policies in the administrative side of the government. And from its stability do we assure the home against unemployment and preserve its security and comfort.

The Protective Tariff

I advocate strengthening of the protective tariff as Henry Clay of Kentucky advocated it; not as an abstract economic theory, but as a practical and definite policy of protecting the standards of living of the American family. The purpose of the tariff is not to balance the books of business corporations but to safeguard the family budget. With the increasing pressures from countries of lower standards of living it has become the fundamental safeguard of the American workman and the American farmer. I wish to see complete protection for the farmer of our home market. It is vital to the South as well as to other parts of the country. It would produce a needed further diversification of Southern agriculture. A retreat would ruin millions of our farmers today.

And likewise the great manufacturing industries of the South are dependent upon it. Your vast spinning industry, your iron and steel industries, are the product of it. No more beneficent exhibit of the result of the Protective Tariff Act passed in 1922 exists than in this very city. Here factories are in course of erection and expansion whose establishment within the United States is due solely to that tariff act. Directly and indirectly they will provide improved livelihood to more than fifteen thousand homes. If it were not for that protection these goods would be imported today as the product of foreign labor.

Agriculture

We must continue our endeavor to restore economic equality to those farm families who have lagged behind in the march of progress.

In the past seven and one-half years Congress has passed more than a score of constructive acts in direct aid of the farmer and the improvement of his marketing system. They have contributed greatly to strengthen the agricultural industry. Our party has undertaken to go farther than this and to still further reorganize farmers' marketing systems, placing it on a basis of greater stability and security. I may repeat these proposals. We stand specifically pledged to create a Federal Farm Board of men sympathetic with the problem, to be clothed with powers and resources with which not only to further aid farmers' co-operatives and assist generally in solving the multitude of different farm problems which arise from all quarters of our nation, but in particular to build up with initial advances of capital from the government farmer-owned and farmer-controlled stabilization corporations which will protect the farmer from depressions and the demoralization of summer and periodic surpluses. Such an instrumentality should be able to develop as years go on the constructive measures necessary to solve the farmers' new problems that will inevitably arise. It is no proposal of subsidy or fee or tax upon the farmer. It is a proposal to assist the farmer on to his own feet into control of his own destinies. This is not a theoretic formula. It is a business proposition designed to make farming more profitable. No such far-reaching and specific proposal has ever been made by a political party on behalf of any industry in our history. It marks our desire for establishment of farmers' stability and at the same time maintains his independence and individuality.

I do not favor any increase in immigration. Restriction protects the American home from widespread unemployment. At the same time we must humanize the laws but only within the present quotas.

Important National Projects

The purpose of the Eighteenth Amendment is to protect the American home. A sacred obligation is imposed on the President to secure its honest enforcement and to eliminate the abuses which have grown up around it; I wish it to succeed.

I believe in continued development of good roads. They bring the farmers' produce to market more cheaply, and by them we gain in neighborly contacts and uplift of spirit.

I advocate the enlarged and vigorous development of our inland waterways because they tend to diversify industry, they cheapen the transportation of farm produce, and they bring larger returns to the farm home.

I rejoice at the enactment of legislation authorizing the construction of flood control works of the Mississippi and other rivers, for they give protection to thousands of homes and open the opportunity for new homes. We should complete these works with the utmost energy.

Because three million of our homes obtain their support from manufacture of articles which we import and export, we must continue to promote and defend our foreign trade.

We must assure a sound merchant marine to safeguard our overseas trade against foreign discrimination.

We must inexorably pursue the present policies of economy in government, for through every tax reduction we leave more income in every home.

It is vital that the government continue its effort to aid in the elimination of waste in production and distribution, through scientific research and by direct cooperation with business. By it we have made great gains in stability. From stability in business come increased consumption of farm products, regularity of employment, and certainty to the family budget.

We must maintain our navy and our army in such fashion that we shall have complete defense of our homes from even the fear of foreign invasion.

Our foreign policies must be ever directed to the cause of peace that we never again need sacrifice our sons on the field of battle.

To our veterans who gave freely of their all in times of danger we must continue to be not only just but generous in enacting and interpreting laws for their relief.

To protect our people from violence at home we must revise our court procedure to produce swifter and surer justice and we should begin with the Federal Government.

I believe in the merit system of the Civil Service, and I believe further that appointive offices must be filled by those who deserve the confidence and respect of the communities they serve.

It is absolutely essential to the moral development and the enlarged opportunity of the boys and girls in every home that we increasingly strengthen our public school system and our institutions of higher learning.

All legislation, all administrative action, must stand the supreme test that it provide equal opportunity for all our citizens, not for any special group.

The Government and Business

I do not favor any general extension of the Federal Government into the operation of business in competition with its citizens. It is not the system of Lincoln or Roosevelt. It is not the American system. It not only undermines initiative but it undermines state and local self-government. It is the destruction of states' rights. Democracy, however, must be master in its own house. It can assure the conservation of our governmentally controlled natural resources in the interest of the people. It has demonstrated that by the power of regulation it can prevent abuse; it can and must control natural monopolies in full public interest. It can do so without abdicating the very principles upon which our nation has been founded and through which we have reached a standard of living and comfort unparalleled in the world. Violations of public interest by individuals or corporations should be followed by the condemnation and punishment they deserve, but this should not induce us to abandon progressive principles and substitute in their place deadly and destructive doctrines. There are local instances where the government must enter the business field as a by-product of some great major purpose, such as improvement in navigation, flood control, scientific research, or national defense; but they do not vitiate the general policy to which we should adhere.

The President has primarily the great task of administering the biggest business in the world—the United States Government. It is a business involving an expenditure of $3,500,000,000 a year and the employment of hundreds of thousands of people. Its honest and efficient administration touches the welfare of our people to a degree perhaps as great as the legislative and political policies. The President also has the responsibility of co-operating with Congress in the enactment of laws and securing their enforcement. In the determination of policies he is not only the leader of a party. He is more than this. He is the President of the whole people. He must interpret the conscience of America. He must guide his conduct by the idealism of our people. The Presidency is no dictatorship. It is not intended to be. Safeguards are provided to prevent it. Our fathers knew that men were not made for government but government for men —to aid and to serve them. Our government rests solely upon the will of the people; it springs from the people; its policies must be approved by the people.

Co-operation, Not Dictation

From my experience in government in the past years both in war and peace I have been profoundly impressed with the fact that we have increasing need to replace dictation by law to the fullest extent possible by co-operation between the administrative side of our government and the forces in the community. Scores of activities organized in these years through co-operation with voluntary bodies on both the economic and welfare sides have convinced me that far more of the problem of progress can be accomplished by voluntary action assisted with co-operation by the government than has been supposed.

One test of our economic and social system is its capacity to cure its own abuses. New abuses and new relationships to the public interest will occur as long as we continue to progress. If we are to be wholly dependent upon government to cure every evil, we shall by this very method have created an enlarged and deadening abuse through the extension of bureaucracy and the clumsy and incapable handling of delicate economic forces. And much abuse has been and can be cured by inspiration and co-operation rather than by regulation of the government.

Basic Integrity of American Life

I have had the good fortune of many journeys to the South and of many warm friendships there. To me came the opportunity of service during the long months of the greatest disaster which has ever come to our own country outside of war—the Mississippi flood. In that service I came to even more fully appreciate not only the character and the devotion of the Southern people, but I found proof of a phase of our American life that I had long believed existed but was difficult of demonstration. I, with other Americans, have perhaps unduly resented the stream of criticism of American life, of the stature and character of our people. More particularly have I resented the sneers at Main Street. For I have known that in the cottages that lay behind the street rested the strength of our national character. When it came to the organization necessary to meet that great catastrophe, the pressure of time alone made it necessary to rely wholly upon the leadership, intelligence, the devotion, the sense of integrity and service of hundreds of towns and villages on the border of the flood. It was they who must undertake the instant work of rescue, the building of gigantic camps, the care of children, the provision of food, the protection of health of three-quarters of a million of homeless people. All that we who were in the direction could do was to outline the nature of the service that every town and village should perform, assist them with resources. In the face of that terrific problem that would test the stamina and quality of any people there was not a failure in a single case. This perhaps stands out larger in my mind than in most men because under similar conditions of great emergency I have had the duty to organize populations abroad. And in no country does there exist the intelligence, the devotion, the probity, the ability to rise to a great emergency that exists in the Main Street of the American town and village. I do not wish to disparage the usefulness of Broadway, Pennsylvania Avenue, or State Street, but it is from Main Street and its countryside that the creative energies of the nation must be replenished and restored.

I rejoice with you at the wonderful development in the South not alone because of the benefits which it has brought but because it represents something more fundamental. Many of our most difficult problems in national life have come because of the extraordinary growth of our great cities. History shows that crowded cities too often breed injustices and crimes, misery and suffering. The people of the South, and of New England especially, are showing the country how to join industry with agriculture to their mutual benefit. The importance of your effort and your success cannot be overstated.

The Federal Government can assist this movement of wider spread of industry by scientific research, by surveys of the resources of each region and study of its interest in and adaptability to various industries. And the government can do more. It can directly assist not only the South but the whole nation in this course by the improvement of our roads, waterways, and ports, and by the encouragement of the spread of electrical power to factory and farm, by building up of the merchant marine, and expansion of the foreign markets natural to each section.

I have endeavored in this address to present to you the policies which have made and will make for prosperity of our country. They hold the hope of the final abolition of poverty. They make for better homes. They make for more individuality in life. They open the door of opportunity to boys and girls of town and country as well as of the great cities. From these accomplishments comes the lift of moral and spiritual life. From them comes an America greater and higher in purpose.

Three halls were filled on the occasion of the Boston address. Mr. Hoover spoke in the Arena, holding eight thousand; overflow meetings were held in Tremont Temple and in Mechanics' Hall. After finishing his address in the Arena, Mr. Hoover repeated parts of it to the crowd in Mechanics' Hall.

BOSTON, MASSACHUSETTS

October 15, 1928

Economic questions have over the past fifty years grown to a larger and larger proportion of our national issues. Today these questions are more dominant than ever. Upon their sound solution depend our prosperity, our standards of living, and the opportunities for a fuller life to every home. I make no apologies therefore for speaking to you tonight on economic questions, as they are affected by the tariff and our foreign trade, including our merchant marine. Obviously the policies of our government bear the most important relationship to the maintenance and expansion of foreign trade, and the government is the sole origin of the tariff.

I have been told that traditionally these subjects are of less interest to the women of our country than to the men. This I do not believe. Not alone are women today a large part of the army of industry, but they are also the treasurers of the household, and the security of the family income is to them of primary concern.

There are no more important questions to the people of New England than this. Nature has given you no coal mines, no oil wells, no vast expanse of prairie—in fact, no great possessions of raw materials. Your transportation relations, both inland and overseas, do not present to you the economic opportunity for basic raw material industries.

New England Concerned with Foreign Trade

But New England has something even more important than all this. It has from the very beginnings of our history provided industrial and commercial leadership and skilled workmanship in the United States. The courage, genius, and lofty integrity of that leadership have for two hundred years carried New England through a score of those inevitable crises that come from invention, from change in demand.

New England began with a shipping industry as her dominant commercial occupation. She succeeded in it because she built better ships, because she was more skillful in ship construction, and because she developed greater skill in operation. She spread her ships over all the seas. She was the first part of our country to develop the factory system. She trained the first skilled workers, erected the first machinery, and set up the first equipment of modern industry. Her people have developed not only a great industry and commerce but a great inheritance of method and skill. It is not simply a great past; it is a great present.

Today, with her reservoir of skilled artisanship, of able technologists and administrators, with her own capital, with access to the markets of our own country and of the world, New England is, and will continue to be over many generations to come, the great American center for production of those articles where we require quality rather than quantity. But the very nature of her location, the character of her industry, and her resources make New England on one hand dependent upon the tariff to protect certain of her industries in the American market, and upon the other hand the development of foreign trade to find world markets for others.

Insures Needed Stable Market

And today the whole nation has more profound reasons for solicitude in the promotion of our foreign trade than ever before. As the result of our inventive genius and the pressure of high wages, we have led the world in substituting machines for hand labor. This, together with able leadership and skilled workers, enables us to produce goods much in excess of our own needs. Taking together our agriculture and our manufactures and our mining, we have increased our production approximately thirty per cent during the last eight years, while our population has increased only about ten per cent. Much of this increase of production has been absorbed in higher standards of living, but the surplus grows with this unceasing improvement. To insure continuous employment and maintain our wages we must find a profitable market for these surpluses.

Nor is this the only reason for lending high importance to our foreign trade, either for New England or the country as a whole. Our business ideal must be stability—that is, regularity of production and regularity of employment. We attain stability in production, whether it be in the individual factory or in the whole industry, or whether it is in the nation at large, by the number of different customers we supply. The shock of decreased demand from a single customer can be absorbed by the increase from another, if distribution be diffused. Consequently our industries will gain in stability, the wider we spread our trade with foreign countries. This additional security reflects itself in the home of every worker and every farmer in our country.

Promotes International Prosperity

The expansion of export trade has a vital importance in still another direction. The goods which we export contribute to the purchase from foreign countries of the goods and raw materials which we cannot ourselves produce. We might survive as a nation, though, on lower living standards and wages, if we had to suppress the nine per cent or ten per cent of our total production which is now sold abroad. But our whole standard of life would be paralyzed and much of the joy of living destroyed if we were denied sufficient imports. Without continued interchange of tropical products with those of the temperate zone, whole sections of the world, including our own country, must stagnate and degenerate in civilization. We could not run an automobile, we could not operate a dynamo or use a telephone, were we without imported raw materials from the tropics. In fact, the whole structure of our advancing civilization would crumble and the great mass of mankind would travel backwards if the foreign trade of the world were to cease. The Great War brought into bold relief the utter dependence of nations upon foreign trade. One of the major strategies of that hour was to crush the enemy by depriving him of foreign trade and therefore of supplies of material and foodstuffs vital to his existence.

Trade in its true sense is not commercial war; it is a vital mutual service. The volume of world trade depends upon prosperity. In fact, it grows from prosperity. Every nation loses by the poverty of another. Every nation gains by the prosperity of another. Our prosperity in the United States has enabled us in eight years to make enormous increases in the purchase of goods from other nations. These increasing purchases have added prosperity and livelihood to millions of people abroad. And their prosperity in turn has enabled them to increase the amount of goods they can buy from us.

Realizing these essentials, one of the first acts of the Republican administration when we came into power seven and one-half years ago—confronted as we were by millions of unemployed—was to devise measures to vigorously restore and expand our foreign trade. It was evident that we must sell more products abroad if we would restore jobs, maintain steady employment for labor and activity for our industries. It was clear that we must dispose of the farmer's surplus abroad if he was to recover stability and an ability to buy the products of our labor. As an aftermath of the war we were confronted with a total disorganization of our export trade. Our exports of war materials had been brought suddenly to an end. But, more than this, the trade of the entire world was demoralized to the extent that the actual movement of commodities between nations was less than before the war. We set out on a definitely organized campaign to build up the export of our products. To accomplish this we reorganized the Department of Commerce on a greater scale than has ever been attempted or achieved by any government in the world. We mobilized our manufacturers and exporters, and co-operated with them in laying out and executing strategic plans for expanding our foreign trade with all nations and in all directions.

The Republican administration by this action introduced a new basis in government relation with business and, in fact, a new relationship of the government with its citizens. That basis was definitely organized co-operation. The method was not dictation nor domination. It was not regulation, nor subsidies, nor other artificial stimulants such as were adopted by foreign nations in similar plight. It was the government, with all its prestige, interested solely in public welfare, acting through trained specialists in voluntary co-operation with committees of business men to promote the interest of the whole country in expansion of its trade and its ultimate expression, which is increased and stable employment. It was the promotion of initiative and enterprise which characterize our business men, and nowhere greater than in New England.

In the year 1922 our foreign trade upon a quantitative basis was almost the same as it was before the war, that is, if we reduce the values by the amount of inflation of the dollar. Since that time our trade has increased steadily year by year until in the year 1927 our exports amounted to the gigantic sum of $4,865,000,000 —or a billion dollars increase under Republican rule. Our imports increased in the past seven years by over $1,675,000,000 to a total of $4,185,000,000. There never have been such increases in a similar period before in our history. Today we are the largest importers and the second largest exporters of goods in the world. Our exports show on a quantitative basis an increase of fifty-eight per cent over pre-war, while our imports are eighty per cent above pre-war. The other combatant nations are only now barely recovering their pre-war basis. All this has a very human interpretation. Our total volume of exports translates itself into employment for 2,400,000 families, while its increase in the last seven years has interpreted itself into livelihood for 500,000 additional families in the United States. And in addition to this, millions more families find employment in the manufacture of imported raw materials. The farmer has a better market for his produce by reason of their employment.

Nor has New England failed to participate fully in this great advance.

Instance from Department of Commerce

With perhaps pardonable pride I may point out some indication of the assistance which the government has given to this great expansion of our export trade through searching out opportunity for American goods abroad. I know of no better index of what the Federal Government's contribution has been in this enormous growth than the number of requests which come constantly to the Department of Commerce from our manufacturers and exporters for assistance and service of one kind or another. During the year before we undertook this broad plan of co-operation the government at its various offices over the world received less than seven hundred such requests per day. These demands have increased steadily until this last fiscal year they exceeded the enormous total of over ten thousand daily. Unless these services to individual manufacturers and exporters were bringing positive results in dollars and cents, we should never have seen this phenomenal growth.

Concern as to Imports

Nor is the government solely concerned with the sale of our products abroad. We are deeply interested in many ways in our imports. One of the most intricate questions has been to secure the supply, at reasonable prices, of raw materials which we do not produce. Beginning soon after the war, certain foreign governments possessing practical monopoly of such materials, began the organization of controls designed to establish prices to the rest of the world, and especially to us, the largest purchaser. These controls increased in number until they embraced nearly one-third of our imports and the undue tax upon our consumers reached hundreds of millions of dollars. We regarded such controls to be in the long run uneconomic and disastrous to the interests of both producer and consumer. We, however, felt we had no complaint except in cases where these methods resulted in speculation and consequent unfair prices to our people. We wish to pay fair price for what we buy just as we wish to secure a fair price for what we sell. It was necessary for us to demonstrate that the consumer has inherent rights. Our government used its influence to assist American industry to meet this situation, by encouraging the use of substitutes and synthetic products, and by recommending public conservation at times of absolute necessity. Happily the trend in the creation and management of these monopolies has reversed itself, and I believe this question will present no further difficulty.

The government bears other direct responsibilities in promoting and safeguarding our foreign trade. It can prosper only under sound financial policies of our government; it can prosper only under improving efficiency of our industry. In fact its progress marches only with the march of all progress, whether it be education or decrease in taxes. Foreign trade thrives only in peace. But, more than that, it thrives only with maintained good will and mutual interest with other nations.

Protection of Citizens Abroad

One of these mutual interests lies in the protection of American citizens and their property abroad, and the protection of foreign citizens in our borders. The world's trading operations are by necessity largely carried on through the agency of their own citizens who migrate to foreign countries. So that in the pursuit of foreign trade we have an exchange of citizens as well as of goods.

Furthermore our citizens who go abroad to develop foreign countries, or our citizens who loan their savings to develop foreign countries, are contributing to the advancement of trade. But they do much more. They build up the standards of living and the prosperity in other countries. Unless there can be constantly evidenced amongst all nations that the lives and property of all citizens abroad shall be protected, the foreign trade and the economic life of the world will degenerate instead of thrive. This does not imply that our citizens going abroad are not subject to the laws of the country where they reside. They must be subject to such laws unless these laws are a violation of international obligation. This implies no imperialism. It is the simple recognition of the principle of comity and mutual interest among all nations. Confidence in this principle is a necessity to the advancement of civilization itself. Fortunately the occasions where it has been necessary to send armed forces to preserve this principle are diminishing. Aside from the Great War the Democratic administration found it necessary to take such action on nine occasions, while during this administration only four such incidents have arisen. Every American must hope that they will not again arise.

Increasing Importance of Government Co-operation

Government co-operation in promoting foreign trade

is even more important for the future than it has been for the past. It is more important to New England than it has ever been before. With the assurance of peace for many years to come, the world is upon the threshold of great commercial expansion. The other great nations of the world have been slowly recovering from the war. They have attained a very large degree of economic stability. They are developing increased efficiency in production and distribution and promotion of trade. Almost every month brings some deputation from abroad to study our methods and processes, which they soon translate into their own use. We do not begrudge them all of our technical and other information. We search with equal diligence to translate their methods of progress to our own use. We have the intelligent self-interest to realize that it is in the prosperity and progress of the world as a whole that we must seek expansion in our foreign trade. Nevertheless, as the stability of foreign nations becomes greater and their methods improve, their competition for neutral markets will become sharper. To receive our due share of prosperity in these markets we must continue an increasing vigorous co-operation from our government.

The Tariff Issue

One of the most important economic issues of this campaign is the protective tariff. The Republican Party has for seventy years supported a tariff designed to give adequate protection to American labor, American industry, and the American farm against foreign competition.

Our opponents, after seventy years of continuous opposition to this Republican doctrine, now seek to convince the American people that they have nothing to fear from tariff revision at their hands. The Democratic platform states that they will revise the duties to a basis of "effective competition." They did this once before. When the Underwood Tariff Bill was introduced to Congress in 1913 the Democratic Ways and Means Committee of the House presented it to the country as a "competitive tariff." That measure was surely not a protective tariff. It greatly reduced the tariffs on American manufactures and it removed almost the whole protection of the agricultural industry. The competition which it provided was competition with foreign wages and standards of living. The Democratic tariff was subjected to test for only a few months prior to the outbreak of the war. Those few months showed the beginnings of disaster in both industry and agriculture. The production of goods abroad competing with our goods ceased during the war and tariff rates became relatively unimportant. It was not until peace was restored that its ill effects were completely disclosed to the American people. It would seem fair to assume from the declarations of the authors of the measure at the time the

Underwood Bill was passed that it was the ideal of an "effective competitive" tariff. Be this as it may, competition, to be effective, must mean that foreign goods will have opportunity of successfully invading our home markets. The effect of the formula there set forth means a reduction of the tariff and a depression in American wages and American farm prices to meet foreign competition. It means a flood of foreign goods, of foreign farm produce, with the consequent reduction of wages and income of not only workers and farmers but the whole of those who labor, whether in the field, at the bench, or at the desk.

The Republican Party stands for protection, and on coming into power in 1922 it enacted again a protective tariff to both agriculture and industry.

Dismal Prophecies Not Fulfilled

Every argument urged by our opponents against the increased duties in the Republican Tariff Act has been refuted by actual experience. It was contended that our costs of production would increase. Their prophecy was wrong, for our costs have decreased. They urged that the duties which we proposed would increase the price of manufactured goods—yet prices have steadily decreased. It was urged that, by removing the pressure of competition of foreign goods, our industry would fall in efficiency. The answer to that is found in our vastly increased production per man in every branch of industry, which, indeed, is the envy of our competitors. They asserted that the enactment of the tariff would reduce the volume of our imports. Yet, during the last seven years, our total imports, particularly of goods which we do not ourselves produce, have greatly increased. They predicted that with decreasing imports it would follow that our sales of goods abroad would likewise decrease. Again they were wrong. Our exports have increased to unprecedented totals. In fact every single argument put forth by our opponents against us at that time has proved to be fallacious.

The tariff written by the Republican Party in 1922 has been accompanied by everything which our opponents predicted that the tariff would prevent. It has been accompanied by employment and prosperity.

Tariff Revision

The Tariff Commission is a most valuable arm of the government. It can be strengthened and made more useful in several ways. But the American people will never consent to delegating authority over the tariff to any commission, whether non-partisan or bi-partisan. Our people have a right to express themselves at the ballot upon so vital a question as this. There is only one commission to which delegation of that authority can be made. That is the great commission of their own choosing, the Congress of the United States and the President. It is the only commission which can be held responsible to the electorate. Those who believe in the protective tariff will, I am sure, wish to leave its revision in the hands of that party which has been devoted to establishment and maintenance of that principle for seventy years.

No tariff act is perfect. With the shifting of economic tides some items may be higher than necessary, but undoubtedly some are too low. This is particularly true so far as New England is concerned. New England has many protected industries. One important branch of them, the cotton and wool industries, have not for the past few years been in a satisfactory condition. They comprise about twenty-six per cent of New England's industrial life. Their depressed condition has not been peculiar to New England. The same situation has prevailed throughout the world and is due largely to the same factors—style changes, production in new areas, and decided changes in the trends of consumption. There has been less hardship in the United States than abroad, and that fact has been due to the partial protection afforded in the tariff against inundations of foreign goods.

Any change in the present policy of protection would, without question, result in a flood of foreign textile products which would mean no less than ruin to New England industry, both manufacturers and workmen.

The Textile Industry

That our American textile industry and its workers need solid protection is clearly demonstrated by a comparison of wages, and it must be remembered that our most severe competition from abroad always comes in those types of cloths in which the element of labor represents the chief item of cost. A woolen and worsted weaver in the United States earns an average of 65 cents an hour, in Great Britain 30 cents, in Germany 20 cents, in France 13 cents, and in Italy 8 cents. The American cotton weaver earns an average of 40 cents an hour, the German 17 cents, the Frenchman less than 11 cents, and the Italian 7 cents an hour. And New England wages are higher than these averages for the whole country. The American protective tariff is the only insurance to our 600,000 families who earn their livelihood in the cotton and wool manufacturing industries against the wages prevalent abroad and the conditions and standards of living which necessarily result from them.

The prospects for the textile industry are today much more favorable than for some time past. Both the world situation and the domestic situation are improving. I believe these industries have turned the corner. And there are omens of much broader significance which sustain me in my beliefs. As never before in the industry there is demonstrated a will to pool its best brain resources in the solution of present and future problems in order that there shall be mutuality of benefit to manufacturer, worker, and consumer. Elimination of waste in production and distribution are in progress. Security and steady employment are more assured than for a long time past.

The Tariff: Theory versus Experience

During this campaign some of our opponents have asserted that it is inconsistent to support the protective tariff and at the same time expect a greater expansion of our foreign trade. Their presentation of this theory at least indicates that some of them have not departed from their long-held free-trade theories.

Their theory is that if by a tariff wall against competitive goods we reduce the sales of goods to us from foreign countries, we thereby diminish the resources of those foreign countries with which to buy goods from us and thus in turn our sales abroad are decreased. It is still further asserted that if we by the tariff reduce the shipment of goods into our markets, then we diminish the ability of foreign countries to pay principal and interest on the debts which they owe us. This theory was sound enough in the old days of direct barter of goods between nations. The trouble with it is that it has lost most of its practical application in a modern world and especially as applied to the American situation. Economic theories and hypotheses must stand the test of fact or experience or show application to new circumstances. Responsible men cannot dally with critical policies which affect the well-being of peoples on the sole basis of a theory. The birth of modern science was the realization by the scientists that every theory and every hypothesis must be placed upon the scales where the weights were in quantities, not arguments.

Foreign Trade Not Barter

One primary fault of this economic theory is that foreign trade is no longer a direct barter between one single nation and another. World trade has become more of the nature of a common pool into which all nations pour goods or credit and from which they retake goods and credit. Let me give you an example: We ship more goods to Great Britain than we receive from her. But we buy vast quantities of tropical goods and she in turn supplies the tropical countries with her manufactures. In this way the settlement of international balances and obligations is lifted entirely out of the category of direct barter.

Bulk of Imports Admitted Free

The first answer, however, to this theory is that sixty-five per cent of our $4,185,000,000 of annual imports are admitted free of duties because they are raw materials, tropical products, and other articles which we do not ourselves produce. Of the remainder, from six per cent to seven per cent are luxuries upon which duties are levied for revenue and which are bought by our people irrespective of price. The purchasing power of foreign countries is certainly undiminished to the extent of this seventy per cent.

Effect of Revenue Paid

A further answer is that thirty per cent, or $1,250,-000,000, of imports came in over the tariff wall and paid duties to the useful revenue of the government of about $470,000,000. The purchasing power for our goods was undiminished by this amount.

Other Foreign Trade Items

A still further answer to this theory opposed to the protective tariff is the enormous increase of what are usually called the "invisibles" of foreign trade, that is, the expenditures for freights, for insurance, by tourists, by immigrant remittances, for interest, and a hundred other items. Some years ago, believing that these transactions were of vastly more importance in the determination of our national policies than had been credited to them, I instituted an annual determination of the facts. These determinations show that foreign nations now receive from us about two billions of dollars per annum for services, including such items as $770,000,000 paid out in foreign countries by our tourists and $240,000,000 remitted by immigrants in our country to relatives abroad. This sum of two billions can be applied by foreigners to the purchase of goods or to payments on debts or for services in the United States just the same as the money which they receive from the sale of goods to us. If we add this two billions to the $4,185,000,000 of goods they sell us, it makes their purchasing power over six billions. So that the proportion of the foreigners' buying power which is affected by the protective tariff diminishes to even a smaller ratio.

Still another answer is that the volume of imports is in fact determined by the degree of prosperity of nations. Our domestic prosperity has been greatly increased by the building up of wages and standards of living, to which the protective tariff has greatly contributed. By the very result of the tariff we have been able vastly to increase our imports of luxuries, raw materials, and things we do not produce. With our domestic prosperity we require more raw materials, and by that same prosperity we have the resources with which to buy them. By our prosperity we have been able to go abroad as tourists and also to remit to our relatives in Europe. This I believe finally extinguishes the already depleted importance of this theory that our tariff seriously damages the buying power of foreign countries and thus diminishes our export trade.

Pertinent Trade Statistics

But if any more answers are needed to this theory there is that of actual practical experience. I have already observed that we have increased our imports during the last seven and one-half years under the present tariff act by over $1,675,000,000 annually, or to an amount at least eighty per cent above pre-war average after allowing for the higher prices. The exports of five leading manufacturing nations of Europe to the United States have increased seventy-five per cent since 1913, whereas the sales of these same nations to the rest of the world have only increased twenty-seven per cent. Certainly that does not indicate any great destruction of their ability to sell us something despite our tariff. In short there is no practical force in the contention that we cannot have a protective tariff and a growing foreign trade. We have both today.

Effect of Loans Abroad

I spoke a few minutes ago of loans which our citizens make to foreign countries. It is an essential part of the sound expansion of our foreign trade that we should interest ourselves in the development of backward or crippled countries by means of loans from our surplus capital. They bring blessings both to the lender and to the borrower. When we make a loan abroad the amount of

payments must ultimately be made in goods and these goods will some day replace the output of our factories and reduce the employment of our workmen. This latter argument has been vigorously put forward as a reason for canceling our war debts. I deny its practical validity.

The whole of the weights which I have applied to the fallacy that the protective tariff ruins our export trade applies equally to this matter. As I have said, the tariff can affect but a small percentage of the buying power of foreign countries. In the end it probably increases imports because by increasing our domestic prosperity it enables us to buy far more goods of the raw material, tropical, and luxury type. All the facts I have stated showing the increased buying power of foreign countries apply equally to their ability to pay loans and interest. The $320,000,000 annually due us upon war debt settlements represents today less than five per cent of the present total annual buying power of foreign countries for our goods and other purposes. Of this five per cent four-fifths would be paid through invisibles as duty-free goods, and only one per cent, at the largest computation, in competitive goods. A hard, practical fact enters here also, which is that their buying power from us is constantly increasing. The fact is, the increase in our tourist expenditure alone in Europe since the war would enable them to take care of the entire amount of their annual payments on these debts. The increase in our imported goods alone since 1922 would pay the whole amount three times over. And the polyangular course of trade which I have mentioned does not require that these transactions be direct with any nation.

War Profits a Fallacy

While I am on this subject of our war debt I should like to call attention to another current misrepresentation. That is the statement that we made a profit from the Great War and that these debts were wrung from the blood of other countries. This is absolutely untrue. While certain individuals may have profited, as a whole this country was a great loser by the war. We emerged from it with the loss of life of our sons, with the depleted health of others, with a huge debt, increased taxes, inflated currency, inflated agriculture, useless factories, with a shortage of housing and other facilities for the very basis of living, with suspended public works and inadequate communications, demoralized railways, and countless other national losses which will continue for a generation.

Prosperity a Post-War Achievement

The increase in wealth and prosperity in the United States has come since the war—not during that time. It is due to the hard-working character and increasing efficiency of our people and to sound government policies.

And in the largest measure the adoption and application of these policies were due to that great son of New England, Calvin Coolidge.

This great prosperity, this great increase in wealth, has been one of the greatest blessings that has ever come to the world. It has enabled us from our reservoir of wealth to contribute the force of our capital to the reconstruction of the war-torn countries. But for our aid South America and many other parts of the world would have been compelled to suspend their development and expansion for lack of capital. Had it not been for the industry and genius of the American people in the last seven years, recovery of the world would have been delayed a quarter of a century.

The American Merchant Marine

A merchant marine under the American flag is an essential to our foreign trade. It is essential to our defense. There is only one protection of our commerce from discrimination and combinations in rates which would impose onerous charges upon us in the transportation of our goods to foreign markets—that is, a merchant marine under the control of our citizens. We have had need to revise our vision of overseas transportation during the past few years. It no longer comprises large numbers of tramp steamers going hither and yon. From the point of view of our commerce it consists of about twenty-five important sea routes which are the extensions to foreign destinations of our inland trade routes, upon which we need regular, ferry-like service of large cargo liner ships. This development of large units and repetitive operation fits with the character of our industrial development and opens wider hope for our return to the sea.

We have endeavored for two generations to find methods for restoration of that prestige on the ocean which New England at one time gave to us. During late years we have tried government ownership and operation. No one can now claim that government operation gives promise of either efficiency or permanence. But by government operation we have maintained our independence and our defense in the meantime. By it we have been able to pioneer the trade routes and to build up substantial flow of goods. Thus far it has been succesful, but at heavy cost. As these routes have gained in strength many of them have been disposed of to successful operation by private enterprise. With the legislation passed by the last Congress through which a number of indirect aids are given to the merchant marine, there is real hope that the government will ultimately be able to retire from competition with its own citizens in the shipping business, but it cannot retire until we are sure that private enterprise can carry the burden and grow in strength. It is a certainty that government operation will always be unsatisfactory. The government cannot operate cheaply; it cannot rid itself of pernicious bureaucracy and politics; it cannot avoid the interminable difficulties and wastes which come from this kind of organization and direct or indirect political pressures. The hope of a substantial merchant marine lies ultimately in the new character of overseas shipping, in the energy and initiative of our citizens with assistance and co-operation of the government. That assistance and co-operation is now being given and must be continued.

Unity of American Interests

Now let me sum up the thought I should like to leave with you. I have talked to you about the tariff, about international trade, the merchant marine, and other economic forces which may, at first glance, seem far removed from our daily lives. I have tried to make the point that these subjects are no longer remote from any one of you. The time may have been, as someone once said, when the tariff was a local issue or foreign trade and shipping concerned only the local seaports. It is so no longer. Touch the tariff on textiles, and North Carolina feels the blighting influence as quickly as Massachusetts. Nor does it stop there. The farmer finds a diminished market in the lessened demand caused by lower wages. Unsettle the credit structure, and it is not Wall Street that suffers most; it is the little bank, the little factory, the little farm, the modest home. A shortage of shipping to the Gulf ports at once decreases prices to the farmer in Kansas, for he must take more expensive routes to foreign markets. The old local decisive issues are largely gone. The present issue is the well-being and comfort and security of the American family and the American home. On that issue my party presents, as proof of its capacity, the record of growing comfort and security of the past seven years.

New England's Contributions to America

I could not as a Californian conclude without a tribute to the large part which New England men have played in the advancement of my state. They pioneered its first commerce. A Boston man, Thomas O. Larkin, was one of the first American consuls in Mexican California, and in large part to his ability and courage was due the peaceful annexation of my state. It was Daniel Webster who moved California's admission to the Union. It was New England men who established our school system and our universities. Today the sons of New England are among the leaders in our public affairs.

Here in New England, American business began, and because the prosperity of industry and commerce affects the life of every man and woman, every boy and girl, I have dealt with it in this address. But there are other things more important. Because I talk of business it does not mean that I place material things above spiritual things. On the contrary, I see prosperity merely as the rich soil from which spiritual virtues as well as education and art and satisfactions in life can grow.

Your founders came to these shores not through lure of gold; not with the ambition to establish great mercantile enterprises; not with the thirst for adventure. Their first objectives were far different and more lofty.

When the necessities of life and of the spirit had been attended to, their first great desire was to advance learning and perpetuate it for posterity. Out of that lofty ambition came the creation of a score of institutions of higher learning. Later the same spirit inspired the establishment of other colleges in order that women might share equally with men in the opportunities of higher education. And from these institutions went forth the men and women who dotted our Western country with colleges and universities which have now become great, and who carried a love of learning that has led our Central and Western states to endow their public schools and universities not with millions of dollars but literally with hundreds of millions.

New England taught us the ways of business. But you gave us something far finer and more precious. You sent us men and women on fire with the passion for truth and service. You set us the first example in patriotism. The early New Englanders cast their lot for liberty in words that can never die, when the people of Roxbury declared: "Our pious fathers died with the pleasing hope that we, their children, should live free. Let none, as they will answer it another day, disturb the ashes of those heroes by selling their birthright." These words did not spring from any consideration of material advantage. Those of our New England citizens who came in later times have caught that spirit and have carried it forward. It has spread its influence to all our country. As a Westerner, I make grateful acknowledgment of our everlasting debt. Your example set the pattern for America's development.

*On October 22 Mr. Hoover spoke in Madison
Square Garden, making his only appearance
in New York.*

NEW YORK CITY

October 22, 1928

THIS campaign now draws near a close. The platforms of the two parties defining principles and offering solutions of various national problems have been presented and are being earnestly considered by our people.

After four months' debate it is not the Republican Party which finds reason for abandonment of any of the principles it has laid down or of the views it has expressed for solution of the problems before the country. The principles to which it adheres are rooted deeply in the foundations of our national life. The solutions which it proposes are based on experience with government and on a consciousness that it may have the responsibility for placing those solutions in action.

In my acceptance speech I endeavored to outline the spirit and ideals by which I would be guided in carrying that platform into administration. Tonight, I will not deal with the multitude of issues which have been already well canvassed. I intend rather to discuss some of those more fundamental principles and ideals upon which I believe the government of the United States should be conducted.

Recent Progress as the Effect of Republican Policies

The Republican Party has ever been a party of progress. I do not need to review its seventy years of constructive history. It has always reflected the spirit of the American people. Never has it done more for the advancement of fundamental progress than during the past seven and one-half years since we took over the government amidst the ruin left by war.

It detracts nothing from the character and energy of the American people, it minimizes in no degree the quality of their accomplishments to say that the policies of the Republican Party have played a large part in recuperation from the war and the building of the magnificent progress which shows upon every hand today. I say with emphasis that without the wise policies which the Republican Party has brought into action during this period, no such progress would have been possible.

Confidence Restored

The first responsibility of the Republican administration was to renew the march of progress from its collapse by the war. That task involved the restoration of confidence in the future and the liberation and stimulation of the constructive energies of our people. It discharged that task. There is not a person within the sound of my voice who does not know the profound progress which our country has made in this period. Every man and woman knows that American comfort, hope, and confidence for the future are immeasurably higher this day than they were seven and one-half years ago.

Constructive Measures Adopted

It is not my purpose to enter upon a detailed recital of the great constructive measures of the past seven and one-half years by which this has been brought about. It is sufficient to remind you of the restoration of employment to the millions who walked your streets in idleness; to remind you of the creation of the budget system; the reduction of six billions of national debt which gave the powerful impulse of that vast sum returned to industry and commerce; the four sequent reductions of taxes and thereby the lift to the living of every family; the enactment of adequate protective tariff and immigration laws which have safeguarded our workers and farmers from floods of goods and labor from foreign countries; the creation of credit facilities and many other aids to agriculture; the building up of foreign trade; the care of veterans; the development of aviation, of radio, of our inland waterways, of our highways; the expansion of scientific research, of welfare activities; the making of safer highways, safer mines, better homes; the spread of outdoor recreation; the improvement in public health and the care of children; and a score of other progressive actions.

Delicacy of the Task

Nor do I need to remind you that government today deals with an economic and social system vastly more intricate and delicately adjusted than ever before. That system now must be kept in perfect tune if we would maintain uninterrupted employment and the high standards of living of our people. The government has come to touch this delicate web at a thousand points. Yearly the relations of government to national prosperity become more and more intimate. Only through keen vision and helpful co-operation by the government has stability in business and stability in employment been maintained during this past seven and one-half years. There always are some localities, some industries, and some individuals who do not share the prevailing prosperity. The task of government is to lessen these inequalities.

Never has there been a period when the Federal Government has given such aid and impulse to the progress of our people, not alone to economic progress but to the development of those agencies which make for moral and spiritual progress.

The American System

But in addition to this great record of contributions of the Republican Party to progress, there has been a further fundamental contribution—a contribution underlying and sustaining all the others—and that is the resistance of the Republican Party to every attempt to inject the government into business in competition with its citizens.

After the war, when the Republican Party assumed administration of the country, we were faced with the problem of determination of the very nature of our national life. During one hundred and fifty years we have builded up a form of self-government and a social system which is peculiarly our own. It differs essentially from all others in the world. It is the American system. It is just as definite and positive a political and social system as has ever been developed on earth. It is founded upon a particular conception of self-government in which decentralized local responsibility is the very base. Further than this, it is founded upon the conception that only through ordered liberty, freedom, and equal opportunity to the individual will his initiative and enterprise spur on the march of progress. And in our insistence upon equality of opportunity has our system advanced beyond all the world.

Suspended by the War

During the war we necessarily turned to the government to solve every difficult economic problem. The government having absorbed every energy of our people for war, there was no other solution. For the preservation

of the state the Federal Government became a centralized despotism which undertook unprecedented responsibilities, assumed autocratic powers, and took over the
business of citizens. To a large degree we regimented
our whole people temporarily into a socialistic state.
However justified in time of war, if continued in peace-
time it would destroy not only our American system but
with it our progress and freedom as well.

When the war closed, the most vital of all issues both
in our own country and throughout the world was
whether governments should continue their war-time
ownership and operation of many instrumentalities of
production and distribution. We were challenged with
a peace-time choice between the American system of
rugged individualism and a European philosophy of dia-
metrically opposed doctrines—doctrines of paternalism
and state socialism. The acceptance of these ideas would
have meant the destruction of self-government through
centralization of government. It would have meant the
undermining of the individual initiative and enterprise
through which our people have grown to unparalleled
greatness.

Restored under Republican Direction

The Republican Party from the beginning resolutely
turned its face away from these ideas and these war
practices. A Republican Congress co-operated with the

154

Democratic administration to demobilize many of our war activities. At that time the two parties were in accord upon that point. When the Republican Party came into full power it went at once resolutely back to our fundamental conception of the state and the rights and responsibilities of the individual. Thereby it restored confidence and hope in the American people, it freed and stimulated enterprise, it restored the government to its position as an umpire instead of a player in the economic game. For these reasons the American people have gone forward in progress while the rest of the world has halted, and some countries have even gone backward. If anyone will study the causes of retarded recuperation in Europe, he will find much of it due to stifling of private initiative on one hand, and overloading of the government with business on the other.

Proposals Now Menacing This System

There has been revived in this campaign, however, a series of proposals which, if adopted, would be a long step toward the abandonment of our American system and a surrender to the destructive operation of governmental conduct of commercial business. Because the country is faced with difficulty and doubt over certain national problems—that is, prohibition, farm relief, and electrical power—our opponents propose that we must thrust government a long way into the businesses which give rise to these problems. In effect, they abandon the tenets of their own party and turn to state socialism as a solution for the difficulties presented by all three. It is proposed that we shall change from prohibition to the state purchase and sale of liquor. If their agricultural relief program means anything, it means that the government shall directly or indirectly buy and sell and fix prices of agricultural products. And we are to go into the hydro-electric power business. In other words, we are confronted with a huge program of government in business.

There is, therefore, submitted to the American people a question of fundamental principle. That is: shall we depart from the principles of our American political and economic system, upon which we have advanced beyond all the rest of the world, in order to adopt methods based on principles destructive of its very foundations? And I wish to emphasize the seriousness of these proposals. I wish to make my position clear; for this goes to the very roots of American life and progress.

Centralization Fatal to Self-Government

I should like to state to you the effect that this projection of government in business would have upon our system of self-government and our economic system. That effect would reach to the daily life of every man and woman. It would impair the very basis of liberty and freedom not only for those left outside the fold of expanded bureaucracy but for those embraced within it.

Let us first see the effect upon self-government. When the Federal Government undertakes to go into commercial business it must at once set up the organization and administration of that business, and it immediately finds itself in a labyrinth, every alley of which leads to the destruction of self-government.

Commercial business requires a concentration of responsibility. Self-government requires decentralization and many checks and balances to safeguard liberty. Our government to succeed in business would need become in effect a despotism. There at once begins the destruction of self-government.

Unwisdom of Government in Business

The first problem of the government about to adventure in commercial business is to determine a method of administration. It must secure leadership and direction. Shall this leadership be chosen by political agencies or shall we make it elective? The hard practical fact is that leadership in business must come through the sheer rise in ability and character. That rise can only take place in the free atmosphere of competition. Competition is closed by bureaucracy. Political agencies are feeble channels through which to select able leaders to conduct commercial business.

157

Government, in order to avoid the possible incompetence, corruption, and tyranny of too great authority in individuals entrusted with commercial business, inevitably turns to boards and commissions. To make sure that there are checks and balances, each member of such boards and commissions must have equal authority. Each has his separate responsibility to the public, and at once we have the conflict of ideas and the lack of decision which would ruin any commercial business. It has contributed greatly to the demoralization of our shipping business. Moreover, these commissions must be representative of different sections and different political parties, so that at once we have an entire blight upon co-ordinated action within their ranks which destroys any possibility of effective administration.

Moreover, our legislative bodies cannot in fact delegate their full authority to commissions or to individuals for the conduct of matters vital to the American people; for if we would preserve government by the people we must preserve the authority of our legislators in the activities of our government.

Thus every time the Federal Government goes into a commercial business, five hundred and thirty-one Senators and Congressmen become the actual board of directors of that business. Every time a state government goes into business one or two hundred state senators and legislators become the actual directors of that business.

Even if they were supermen and if there were no politics in the United States, no body of such numbers could competently direct commercial activities; for that requires initiative, instant decision, and action. It took Congress six years of constant discussion to even decide what the method of administration of Muscle Shoals should be.

When the Federal Government undertakes to go into business, the state governments are at once deprived of control and taxation of that business; when a state government undertakes to go into business, it at once deprives the municipalities of taxation and control of that business. Municipalities, being local and close to the people, can, at times, succeed in business where federal and state governments must fail. We have trouble enough with log-rolling in legislative bodies today. It originates naturally from desires of citizens to advance their particular section or to secure some necessary service. It would be multiplied a thousandfold were the federal and state governments in these businesses.

The effect upon our economic progress would be even worse. Business progressiveness is dependent on competition. New methods and new ideas are the outgrowth of the spirit of adventure, of individual initiative, and of individual enterprise. Without adventure there is no progress. No government administration can rightly take chances with taxpayers' money.

There is no better example of the practical incompetence of government to conduct business than the history of our railways. During the war the government found it necessary to operate the railways. That operation continued until after the war. In the year before being freed from government operation they were not able to meet the demands for transportation. Eight years later we find them under private enterprise transporting fifteen per cent more goods and meeting every demand for service. Rates have been reduced by fifteen per cent and net earnings increased from less than one per cent on their valuation to about five per cent. Wages of employees have improved by thirteen per cent. The wages of railway employees are today one hundred and twenty-one per cent above pre-war, while the wages of government employees are today only sixty-five per cent above pre-war. That should be a sufficient commentary upon the efficiency of government operation.

Dangers of Bureaucracy

Let us now examine this question from the point of view of the person who may get a government job and is admitted into the new bureaucracy. Upon that subject let me quote from a speech of that great leader of labor, Samuel Gompers, delivered in Montreal in 1920, a few years before his death. He said:

"I believe there is no man to whom I would take

second position in my loyalty to the Republic of the United States, and yet I would not give it more power over the individual citizenship of our country. . . . .

"It is a question of whether it shall be government ownership or private ownership under control. . . . . If I were in the minority of one in this convention, I would want to cast my vote so that the men of labor shall not willingly enslave themselves to government authority in their industrial effort for freedom. . . . .

"Let the future tell the story of who is right or who is wrong; who has stood for freedom and who has been willing to submit their fate industrially to the government."

I would amplify Mr. Gompers' statement. The great body of government employees which would be created by the proposals of our opponents would either comprise a political machine at the disposal of the party in power, or, alternatively, to prevent this, the government by stringent civil-service rules must debar its employees from their full political rights as free men. It must limit them in the liberty to bargain for their own wages, for no government employee can strike against his government and thus against the whole people. It makes a legislative body with all its political currents their final employer and master. Their bargaining does not rest upon economic need or economic strength but on political potence.

But what of those who are outside the bureaucracy? What is the effect upon their lives?

The area of enterprise and opportunity for them to strive and rise is at once limited.

The government in commercial business does not tolerate amongst its customers the freedom of competitive reprisals to which private business is subject. Bureaucracy does not tolerate the spirit of independence; it spreads the spirit of submission into our daily life and penetrates the temper of our people not with the habit of powerful resistance to wrong but with the habit of timid acceptance of irresistible might.

Fatal to True Liberalism

Bureaucracy is ever desirous of spreading its influence and its power. You cannot extend the mastery of the government over the daily working life of a people without at the same time making it the master of the people's souls and thoughts. Every expansion of government in business means that government in order to protect itself from the political consequences of its errors and wrongs is driven irresistibly without peace to greater and greater control of the nation's press and platform. Free speech does not live many hours after free industry and free commerce die.

It is a false liberalism that interprets itself into the government operation of commercial business. Every step of bureaucratizing of the business of our country poisons the very roots of liberalism—that is, political equality, free speech, free assembly, free press, and equality of opportunity. It is the road not to more liberty, but to less liberty. Liberalism should be found not striving to spread bureaucracy but striving to set bounds to it. True liberalism seeks all legitimate freedom first in the confident belief that without such freedom the pursuit of all other blessings and benefits is vain. That belief is the foundation of all American progress, political as well as economic.

Liberalism is a force truly of the spirit, a force proceeding from the deep realization that economic freedom cannot be sacrificed if political freedom is to be preserved. Even if governmental conduct of business could give us more efficiency instead of less efficiency, the fundamental objection to it would remain unaltered and unabated. It would destroy political equality. It would increase rather than decrease abuse and corruption. It would stifle initiative and invention. It would undermine the development of leadership. It would cramp and cripple the mental and spiritual energies of our people. It would extinguish equality and opportunity. It would dry up the spirit of liberty and progress. For these reasons primarily it must be resisted. For a hundred and fifty years liberalism has found its true spirit in the American system, not in the European systems.

I do not wish to be misunderstood in this statement. I am defining a general policy. It does not mean that our government is to part with one iota of its national resources without complete protection to the public interest. I have already stated that where the government is engaged in public works for purposes of flood control, of navigation, of irrigation, of scientific research or national defense, or in pioneering a new art, it will at times necessarily produce power or commodities as a by-product. But they must be a by-product of the major purpose, not the major purpose itself.

Nor do I wish to be misinterpreted as believing that the United States is free-for-all and devil-take-the-hindmost. The very essence of equality of opportunity and of American individualism is that there shall be no domination by any group or combination in this republic, whether it be business or political. On the contrary, it demands economic justice as well as political and social justice. It is no system of laissez faire.

I feel deeply on this subject because during the war I had some practical experience with governmental operation and control. I have witnessed not only at home but abroad the many failures of government in business. I have seen its tyrannies, its injustices, its destructions of self-government, its undermining of the very instincts which carry our people forward to progress. I have witnessed the lack of advance, the lowered standards of living, the depressed spirits of people working under such a system. My objection is based not upon theory or upon a failure to recognize wrong or abuse, but I know the adoption of such methods would strike at the very roots of American life and would destroy the very basis of American progress.

Our people have the right to know whether we can continue to solve our great problems without abandonment of our American system. I know we can. We have demonstrated that our system is responsive enough to meet any new and intricate development in our economic and business life. We have demonstrated that we can meet any economic problem and still maintain our democracy as master in its own house, and that we can at the same time preserve equality of opportunity and individual freedom.

Practicability of Regulation

In the last fifty years we have discovered that mass production will produce articles for us at half the cost they required previously. We have seen the resultant growth of large units of production and distribution. This is big business. Many businesses must be bigger, for our tools are bigger, our country is bigger. We now build a single dynamo of a hundred thousand horsepower. Even fifteen years ago that would have been a big business all by itself. Yet today advance in production requires that we set ten of these units together in a row.

The American people from bitter experience have a rightful fear that great business units might be used to dominate our industrial life and by illegal and unethical practices destroy equality of opportunity.

Years ago the Republican administration established the principle that such evils could be corrected by regulation. It developed methods by which abuses could be prevented while the full value of industrial progress could be retained for the public. It insisted upon the principle that when great public utilities were clothed with the security of partial monopoly, whether it be railways, power plants, telephones, or what not, then there must be the fullest and most complete control of rates, services, and finances by government or local agencies. It declared that these businesses must be conducted with glass pockets.

As to our great manufacturing and distributing industries, the Republican Party insisted upon the enactment of laws that not only would maintain competition but would destroy conspiracies to destroy the smaller units or dominate and limit the equality of opportunity amongst our people.

One of the great problems of government is to determine to what extent the government shall regulate and control commerce and industry and how much it shall leave it alone. No system is perfect. We have had many abuses in the private conduct of business. That every good citizen resents. It is just as important that business keep out of government as that government keep out of business.

Nor am I setting up the contention that our institutions are perfect. No human ideal is ever perfectly attained, since humanity itself is not perfect.

The wisdom of our forefathers in their conception that progress can only be attained as the sum of the accomplishment of free individuals has been reinforced by all of the great leaders of the country since that day. Jackson, Lincoln, Cleveland, McKinley, Roosevelt, Wilson, and Coolidge have stood unalterably for these principles.

Effectiveness of the American System

And what have been the results of our American system? Our country has become the land of opportunity to those born without inheritance, not merely because of the wealth of its resources and industry but because of this freedom of initiative and enterprise. Russia has natural resources equal to ours. Her people are equally industrious, but she has not had the blessings of one hundred and fifty years of our form of government and of our social system.

By adherence to the principles of decentralized self-government, ordered liberty, equal opportunity, and freedom to the individual, our American experiment in human welfare has yielded a degree of well-being unparalleled in all the world. It has come nearer to the abolition of poverty, to the abolition of fear of want, than humanity has ever reached before. Progress of the past seven years is the proof of it. This alone furnishes the answer to our opponents, who ask us to introduce destructive elements into the system by which this has been accomplished.

Let us see what this system has done for us in our recent years of difficult and trying reconstruction and then solemnly ask ourselves if we now wish to abandon it.

Post-War Recovery

As a nation we came out of the war with great losses. We made no profits from it. The apparent increases in wages were at that time fictitious. We were poorer as a nation when we emerged from the war. Yet during these last eight years we have recovered from these losses and increased our national income by over one-third, even if we discount the inflation of the dollar. That there has been a wide diffusion of our gain in wealth and income is marked by a hundred proofs. I know of no better test of the improved conditions of the average family than the combined increase in assets of life and industrial insurance, building and loan associations, and savings deposits. These are the savings banks of the average man. These agencies alone have in seven years increased by nearly one hundred per cent to the gigantic sum of over fifty billions of dollars, or nearly one-sixth of our whole national wealth. We have increased in home ownership, we have expanded the investments of the average man.

Higher Standards of Living

In addition to these evidences of larger savings, our people are steadily increasing their spending for higher standards of living. Today there are almost nine automobiles for each ten families, where seven and one-half years ago only enough automobiles were running to average less than four for each ten families. The slogan of progress is changing from the full dinner pail to the full garage. Our people have more to eat, better things to wear, and better homes. We have even gained in elbow room, for the increase of residential floor space is over twenty-five per cent, with less than ten per cent increase in our number of people. Wages have increased, the cost of living has decreased. The job of every man and woman has been made more secure. We have in this short period decreased the fear of poverty, the fear of unemployment, the fear of old age; and these are fears that are the greatest calamities of humankind.

All this progress means far more than increased

creature comforts. It finds a thousand interpretations into a greater and fuller life. A score of new helps save the drudgery of the home. In seven years we have added seventy per cent to the electric power at the elbows of our workers and further promoted them from carriers of burdens to directors of machines. We have steadily reduced the sweat in human labor. Our hours of labor are lessened; our leisure has increased. We have expanded our parks and playgrounds. We have nearly doubled our attendance at games. We pour into outdoor recreation in every direction. The visitors at our national parks have trebled and we have so increased the number of sportsmen fishing in our streams and lakes that the longer time between bites is becoming a political issue. In these seven and one-half years the radio has brought music and laughter, education and political discussion to almost every fireside.

Springing from our prosperity with its greater freedom, its vast endowment of scientific research, and the greater resources with which to care for public health, we have according to our insurance actuaries during this short period since the war lengthened the average span of life by nearly eight years. We have reduced infant mortality, we have vastly decreased the days of illness and suffering in the life of every man and woman. We have improved the facilities for the care of the crippled and helpless and deranged.

Educational Progress

From our increasing resources we have expanded our educational system in eight years from an outlay of twelve hundred millions to twenty-seven hundred millions of dollars. The education of our youth has become almost our largest and certainly our most important activity. From our greater income and thus our ability to free youth from toil we have increased the attendance in our grade schools by fourteen per cent, in our high schools by eighty per cent, and in our institutions of higher learning by ninety-five per cent. Today we have more youth in these institutions of higher learning twice over than all the rest of the world put together. We have made notable progress in literature, in art, and in public taste.

We have made progress in the leadership of every branch of American life. Never in our history was the leadership in our economic life more distinguished in its abilities than today, and it has grown greatly in its consciousness of public responsibility. Leadership in our professions and in moral and spiritual affairs of our country was never of a higher order. And our magnificent educational system is bringing forward a host of recruits for the succession to this leadership.

I do not need to recite more figures and more evidence. I cannot believe that the American people wish to abandon or in any way to weaken the principles of economic freedom and self-government which have been maintained by the Republican Party and which have produced results so amazing and so stimulating to the spiritual as well as to the material advance of the nation.

Significance to New York City

Your city has been an outstanding beneficiary of this great progress and of these safeguarded principles. With its suburbs it has, during the last seven and one-half years, grown by over a million and a half of people until it has become the largest metropolitan district of all the world. Here you have made abundant opportunity not only for the youth of the land but for the immigrant from foreign shores. This city is the commercial center of the United States. It is the commercial agent of the American people. It is a great organism of specialized skill and leadership in finance, industry, and commerce which reaches every spot in our country. Its progress and its beauty are the pride of the whole American people. It leads our nation in its benevolences to charity, to education, and to scientific research. It is the center of art, music, literature, and drama. It has come to have a more potent voice than any other city in the United States.

But when all is said and done, the very life, progress, and prosperity of this city is wholly dependent on the prosperity of the 115,000,000 people who dwell in our mountains and valleys across the three thousand miles to the Pacific Ocean. Every activity of this city is sensitive to every evil and every favorable tide that sweeps this great nation of ours. Be there a slackening of industry in any place, it affects New York far more than any other part of the country. In a time of depression one-quarter of all the unemployed in the United States can be numbered in this city. In a time of prosperity the citizens of the great interior of our country pour into your city for business and entertainment at the rate of one hundred and fifty thousand a day. In fact, so much is this city the reflex of the varied interests of our country that the concern of every one of your citizens for national stability, for national prosperity, for national progress, for preservation of our American system is far greater than that of any other single part of our country.

Unfinished Tasks

We still have great problems if we would achieve the full economic advancement of our country. In these past few years some groups in our country have lagged behind others in the march of progress. I refer more particularly to those engaged in the textile, coal, and agricultural industries. We can assist in solving these problems by co-operation of our government. To the agricultural industry we shall need to advance initial capital to assist them to stabilize their industry. But this proposal implies that they shall conduct it themselves, and not the government. It is in the interest of our cities that we shall bring agriculture and all industries into full stability and prosperity. I know you will gladly co-operate in the faith that in the common prosperity of our country lies its future.

In bringing this address to a conclusion I should like to restate to you some of the fundamental things I have endeavored to bring out.

The Coming Decision Fundamental

The foundations of progress and prosperity are dependent as never before upon the wise policies of government, for government now touches at a thousand points the intricate web of economic and social life.

Under administration by the Republican Party in the last seven and one-half years our country as a whole has made unparalleled progress and this has been in generous part reflected to this great city. Prosperity is no idle expression. It is a job for every worker; it is the safety and the safeguard of every business and every home. A continuation of the policies of the Republican Party is fundamentally necessary to the further advancement of this progress and to the further building up of this prosperity.

I have dwelt at some length on the principles of relationship between the government and business. I make no apologies for dealing with this subject. The first necessity of any nation is the smooth functioning of the vast business machinery for employment, feeding, clothing, housing, and providing luxuries and comforts to a people. Unless these basic elements are properly organized and function, there can be no progress in business, in education, literature, music, or art. There can be no advance in the fundamental ideals of a people. A people cannot make progress in poverty.

I have endeavored to present to you that the greatness of America has grown out of a political and social system and a method of control of economic forces distinctly its own—our American system—which has carried this great experiment in human welfare farther than ever before in all history. We are nearer today to the ideal of the abolition of poverty and fear from the lives of men and women than ever before in any land. And I again repeat that the departure from our American system by injecting principles destructive to it which our opponents propose will jeopardize the very liberty and freedom of our people, will destroy equality of opportunity not alone to ourselves but to our children.

The New Day

To me the foundation of American life rests upon the home and the family. I read into these great economic forces, these intricate and delicate relations of the government with business and with our political and social life, but one supreme end—that we reinforce the ties that bind together the millions of our families, that we strengthen the security, the happiness, and the independence of every home.

My conception of America is a land where men and women may walk in ordered freedom in the independent conduct of their occupations; where they may enjoy the advantages of wealth, not concentrated in the hands of the few but spread through the lives of all; where they build and safeguard their homes, and give to their children the fullest advantages and opportunities of American life; where every man shall be respected in the faith that his conscience and his heart direct him to follow; where a contented and happy people, secure in their liberties, free from poverty and fear, shall have the leisure and impulse to seek a fuller life.

Some may ask where all this may lead beyond mere material progress. It leads to a release of the energies of men and women from the dull drudgery of life to a wider vision and a higher hope. It leads to the opportunity for greater and greater service, not alone from man to man in our own land, but from our country to the whole world. It leads to an America, healthy in body, healthy in spirit, unfettered, youthful, eager—with a vision searching beyond the farthest horizons, with an open mind, sympathetic and generous. It is to these higher ideals and for these purposes that I pledge myself and the Republican Party.

The last long address of the campaign was given in the Coliseum at St. Louis. Mr. Hoover stopped here, on his way to his Palo Alto home to cast his ballot.

ST. LOUIS, MISSOURI

November 2, 1928

I PROPOSE tonight to discuss the constructive side of government. I propose to outline something of the principles which must underlie the relation of government to the constructive tasks which confront us. A few nights ago in New York I had occasion to discuss these principles in application to matters which the government should not undertake. Tonight I discuss them in connection with matters which the government should and must undertake. Government is only in part a negative function. Its purpose is not merely to stand as a watchman over what is forbidden; government must be a constructive force.

The Unique American System

Our country has a political, social, and economic system that is peculiarly our own. It is the American system. It grew out of our revolt from European systems and has ripened with our experience and our ideals. We have seldom tried to express it or define it. It has been the moving force of our progress. It has brought us into the leadership of the world.

The founders of our republic under Divine inspiration set up not alone a great political system of self-government, but they set up also a revolutionary social system in the relation of men toward men.

Our political system is unique in the world. It is unique because of its decentralization of self-government and its checks and balances which safeguard ordered liberty and freedom to each individual. Our social system is unique in the world. It is unique because it is founded not only upon the ideal that all men are created equal and are equal before the law, but also upon the ideal that there shall be equal opportunity among men. We have no frozen classes or stratification of caste in our country. We allow nothing to prevent the rise of every boy and girl to the position to which their initiative and talents will carry them. We have no titles except the descriptions of our jobs.

From our unique political and social ideals we are evolving a unique economic system. We have discarded the original European theory that there is a class struggle between the capital of the few and the labor of the many. Under that theory it was held that labor was a commodity and the laborer in general could never rise far above bare existence, for if he did so the supply of labor would increase and thus constantly pull him back into the cesspool of inevitable poverty.

We Americans have proved this conception wrong.

By what amounts to a revolution in ideas and methods, we have developed a new economic system. The dominating idea of that system is that labor on the one hand and capital, which in America means the savings of the people, on the other hand, by joint effort can steadily increase the efficiency of production and distribution. In other words, we find that by joint effort we can steadily increase the production of goods by each individual and we can at the same time decrease the cost of goods. As we increase the volume of goods, we have more to divide, and we thereby steadily lift the standard of living of the whole people. We have proved this to be true, and by this proof we have laid away the old theory of inevitable poverty alongside the theory of human slavery.

These three revolutionary American ideas, political, social, and economic, are interlocked and intermeshed. They are dominated and cemented by the ideal and practice of equal opportunity. They constitute one great system protecting our individualism and stimulating initiative and enterprise in our people. This is the American system. One part of it cannot be destroyed without undermining the whole. For us to adopt other social conceptions, such as federal or state government entry into commercial business in competition with its citizens, would undermine initiative and enterprise and destroy the very foundations of freedom and progress upon which the American system is builded.

Aptness of Republican Party Principles

By adhering to these principles the Republican Party has played a large part in creating the magnificent progress which shows on every hand today. I do not need to recite the evidences of that progress. I have said before that it in no way minimizes the accomplishments of the American people to point out that without the wise policies which the Republican Party has made effective during the past seven and one-half years the great prosperity we now enjoy would not have been possible. The Republican Party has ever been a party of true progressivism— true progressivism does not include policies which would destroy progress.

By adhering to these principles we have raised humanity to greater heights of well-being than ever before in history. They are the very essence of progressive government and of self-government. We must apply them to the constructive side of government.

Constructive Government

There are three potential fields in which the principles and impulses of our American system require that government take constructive action. They comprise those activities which no local community can itself assume and which the individual initiative and enterprise of our people cannot wholly compass. They comprise leadership of the government to solve many difficult problems.

The first of these fields includes the great undertakings in public works such as inland waterways, flood control, reclamation, highways, and public buildings.

The second of these is the necessary interest and activity of the Federal Government in fostering education, public health, scientific research, public parks, conservation of national resources, agriculture, industry, and foreign commerce.

The third great field lies in broadening the assistance of the government to the growing efforts of our people to co-operation among themselves to useful social and economic ends.

The first of the particular tasks to which I believe this constructive side of government should be directed is public works.

The Mississippi System

More than any other section of our country the Midwest is at this time vitally concerned with the advancement of these undertakings. I have stated on other occasions that, due to the shift of economic currents from the war, the Midwest has not had equal opportunity with the rest of our country. The natural increase in freight rates due to the war, the building of the Panama Canal, coincident with the fact that the cost of ocean transportation has remained practically stationary, have contributed to thrust the Midwest into an economic setting greatly to her disadvantage.

Almost exactly three years ago at Kansas City I said that this shifting of economic currents demanded a new vision of interior waterway development. I then urged that it was time to reject the old view of inland waterways as a series of isolated projects, and that instead we should consolidate our interior waterways into a great integrated system which I called the Mississippi System.

We have an opportunity to create three great trunk lines of water transportation—one north and south fifteen hundred miles from New Orleans through St. Louis to Chicago, and thus by the Lakes to the northern boundaries of our country. Another east and west sixteen hundred miles from Pittsburgh through St. Louis to Kansas City. And the third a shipway through the St. Lawrence connecting Duluth and all the lake ports with the sea. Vital to this system is the improvement of the laterals such as the upper Mississippi connecting Minneapolis and St. Paul, the upper Missouri connecting Sioux City and beyond, as well as the Cumberland, the Tennessee, the Arkansas, and the Red rivers, and lesser streams. When completed, including the St. Lawrence waterway, this entire system will comprise twelve thousand miles of most essential transportation connecting twenty states with the Gulf on one hand and with the North Atlantic on the other.

Under the direction of Midwest Senators and Congressmen and supported by great civic associations of the

Midwest, and with the help given by the Departments of War and Commerce, that conception of our waterway system has now been finally accepted by the country as a great program for national development. Congress has authorized the completion of the system—except the St. Lawrence, concerning which negotiation with Canada is still pending. We have already expended nearly $100,000,000 upon the new program. It is money well spent.

This comprehensive system will not reach full usefulness until it is complete and interconnected. And it is for that reason that I believe it should be completed at the earliest possible moment. When finished it will be a powerful stimulus to the industry of this great section. It means cheaper raw materials, it means cheaper access to the world market for the Midwest; it means the building of industry in the midst of agriculture; it means the improvement of our whole national economy by bringing the consumer and the producer closer together; and it means a vital contribution to the stability of both industry and agriculture. In a measure it will restore the field of our Midwest merchants, who suffer today by competition through the Panama Canal. By cheapening transportation it will increase the price the farmer receives for his products. This increase constitutes a most important element of his profits. He would obtain this increase not alone upon the actual products that may be transported by these waterways but upon his whole crop. The reason is that the price the farmer receives for certain of his products is the world market price less the cost of transportation; and when parts of his crops can be exported at reduced cost, it compels buyers to enhance the price paid to him for his entire production even though most of it be for domestic consumption.

Nor will this impair our magnificent railway system. The growth of traffic in our country will far outstrip the volume which our waterways will carry.

Any engineer, presented with the conclusive advantage of construction of a great works and having the resources with which it can be constructed, has only one conception of it—its earliest possible completion in order that the returns of the works may be quickly brought into being.

No one could have occupied the position and responsibilities which were assigned to me during the great Mississippi flood of eighteen months ago and not have become an advocate of adequate flood control. I rejoice at the enactment by Congress of authority to construct these works. The safety of over a million and a half of our people depends upon them. We have already witnessed the temporary shock that came to the prosperity of the whole nation through that great disaster. Here again is a necessity for all of the energy which can be applied without waste in order that we shall open its wealth of production to the future and that we shall at the earliest moment remove fear from the hearts of all those who dwell in the great Lower Valley. I am for its completion at the earliest moment.

Federal Highways

This administration has recognized the public necessity of Federal Government contribution to the creation of a definitive system of modern interstate highways. This program is far from completion, and I stand for its continuance. Congress has lately authorized a large program of much-needed public buildings. And there are other important public works of less immediate interest to the Midwest to which I have referred upon other occasions. The whole comprises the largest engineering construction ever undertaken by any government. It means an expenditure of nearly a billion of dollars in the next four years, or nearly four times the outlay on the Panama Canal. As I have said before, these undertakings are justified by the growth, the need, and the wealth of our country. The organization and administration of this construction is a responsibility of the first order. For it we must secure the utmost economy, honesty, and skill. These works, which will provide jobs for an army of men, should, so far as practicable, be adjusted to take up the slack of unemployment if it should occur.

Agriculture

There has never been a national campaign into which so large a discussion of the agricultural problem has entered as in this campaign. That is as it should be. It is the most urgent economic problem in our nation today. It must be solved if we are to bring equality of opportunity and assurance of complete stability of prosperity to all of our people.

I have discussed elsewhere the causes which have led to distress in agriculture. Even before the war it was not on a satisfactory basis, and all discussion which deals with putting it back on a pre-war basis takes us nowhere. There was then a fundamental difficulty which still exists —the undue effect of seasonal and periodic surpluses upon the price. The catastrophic deflation of 1920 was added to by the fact that the Underwood Tariff had removed protection on practically all farm products. In the year of deflation—that is, the year before the Republican Party came into power and was able to give remedy —agricultural products to the amount of three billion dollars poured into the country from abroad and helped break prices already under strain from deflation.

There are many other causes: increased freight rates; increased production abroad; and changes in our production methods at home. There has been a most amazing growth in efficiency of the farmers themselves, who have within eight years increased our production of all farm products about twenty per cent with fewer people employed in the industry and with about the same acreage. This is the answer to any claim that our farmers are not doing their part in the industrial advance. But this increased efficiency has not brought them the same rewards as have come to other professions and callings. The others have marched far ahead of their pre-war basis in standards of living and in comfort, while some branches of agriculture still base their hopes on a restoration of pre-war conditions.

Progress Made under Republican Leadership

There are, therefore, ample causes for complaint. The Republican Party has throughout the whole of the last seven and one-half years been alive to this situation. It has undertaken a long series of measures of assistance. The tariff protection, the revival of the War Finance Corporation, the expansion of Federal Farm Banks, the establishment of Intermediate Credit Banks, the co-operative marketing legislation, the regulation of grain exchanges and stockyards, together with a score of other constructive legislative and administrative efforts, evidence the interest in the farmers' difficulties. Certain branches of the agricultural industry have made substantial progress. Important branches still lag behind, and the problem is as yet unsolved as a whole.

Complexity of the Problem

There have been many reasons for the difficulty of finding a complete solution. Let me offer two or three suggestions. The first is, there has been a tendency to look for solution of the whole agricultural problem with a single formula. The result has been that the leaders of those branches of agriculture to which that formula would not apply or to which it did damage have immediately fallen into opposition. Therefore on any special plan of relief we have always had sharp disagreement within the industry itself.

The depression in different branches of farming comes from widely different sources and has a wide variety of causes. The industry is not a single industry but is a dozen specialized industries absolutely different in their whole economic relationships. If we would have sound and permanent relief, it can be only through complete determination of the causes which bring about the difficulties of each part. By thus going to the root of the trouble we will find that the methods of solution are not through one line of action but through many lines of action.

And the problem is not wholly an economic problem. It is partly a social problem because the farm is more than a place of business—it is a place of living and a home. So that in addition to finding the solution to the particular difficulty in that particular branch of the business, we must have regard for important social problems involved. The whole foundation and hope of our nation is the maintained individualism of our people. Farming is, and must continue to be, an individualistic business of small units and independent ownership. The farmer is the outstanding example of the economically free individual. He is one of our solid materials of national character. No solution that makes for consolidation into large farms and mechanized production can fit into our national hopes and ideals.

Factors in Its Solution

Many factors enter into a solution of this whole problem. One is by the tariff to reserve to the farmer the American market, to safeguard him from the competition of imports of farm products from countries of lower standards of living. Another part of the solution is to provide cheaper transportation to market. Another is to secure to the farmer a larger proportion of the price which the ultimate consumer pays through the elimination of a vast number of wastes that lie in our method of distribution. Another part of the solution must be to secure greater stability in prices which are now unduly affected both by the seasonal surplus and by the periodical surplus over one year to another. Another part of the solution is to maintain stability and high purchasing power for our consumers. Any depression or ill wind which affects the consumer's buying power is immediately reflected to the farmer. Finally, every different agricultural product is affected by different forces, and we must produce a plan of action which will give aid to each as is required.

The Protective Tariff

Adequate tariff is essential if we would assure relief to the farm. The first and most complete necessity is that the American farmer have the American market. That can be assured to him solely through the protective tariff. The tariff is effective today on many farm crops, including wool, flax, sugar, fruit, cattle, dairy products, vegetable oils, and a score of other products. It maintains the premium upon our hard wheat against Canadian imports. The duties are not high enough on some products, but nevertheless the tariff is effective over a considerable portion of our whole agricultural production. And it can be made more effective, for we are still importing something like eight hundred million dollars per annum of products which could be produced on our soil. One difficulty in our present corn market is the imports of corn to our seaboard points. The tariff wall we erect creates also a profitable pressure to diversify the crop and thereby decrease the surplus problem. The increase in dairying and flax-raising, for example, has displaced what would otherwise have been larger and even more unmanageable surpluses of other products.

And beyond this the tariff in protecting the wage level of the American worker increases his buying power for the products of the farmer. Our manufacturing industries of the Midwest require protection from lower wages of foreign countries just as much as those on the seaboard. The standard of living amongst our workers, our city populations, is the only standard in the world which permits them to purchase all the food they can eat. The butter consumption in our country has increased by fifty per cent in eight years, although the population has increased by only ten per cent. The tariff holds butter prices today twelve cents per pound over the prices which prevail in Europe.

And while I am on the tariff and before we turn to other phases of the farm problem, let me say that the party which by the Underwood Bill removed practically all agricultural products from tariff protection, which withheld that protection for two years after the war, which opposed the Republican tariff on agricultural products, and which as late as nine months ago provided only two votes in the Senate and seven votes in the House to defeat a resolution providing for instant tariff reduction—that party is not the party for the American farmer and the American workman to entrust with revision of the tariff. If you want the protective principle preserved, and if you want it strengthened on farm products, it should be entrusted to the party that has fought for and defended it for seventy years.

Immigration

I may also add upon the subject of protection that the limitation of immigration is a fundamental part of our protective system because it prevents a flood of labor from abroad which can only break down our wage levels. I stand against any increase of the present quotas and for the principle of the 1890 census, with only such changes as prevent separation of families but would not increase total numbers.

But to return to the farm question.

A Federal Farm Board

In addition to the tariff and cheaper waterway transportation in assistance to agriculture, the Republican Party proposes to go farther. It proposes to set up an institution which will be one of the most important institutions in our government, designed to meet not only the varied problems which confront us today but those which may arise in the future. We propose to create a Federal Farm Board composed of men of understanding and sympathy for the problems of agriculture; we propose that this board should have power to determine the facts, the causes, the remedies which should be applied to each and every one of the multitude of problems which we mass under the general term "the agricultural problem."

This program further provides that the board shall have a broad authority to act and be authorized to assist in the further development of co-operative marketing; that it shall assist in the development of clearing-houses for agricultural products, in the development of adequate warehousing facilities, in the elimination of wastes in distribution, and in the solution of other problems as they arise. But in particular the board is to build up, with initial advances of capital from the government, farmer-owned and farmer-controlled stabilization corporations which will protect the farmer from depressions and the demoralization of summer and periodic surpluses.

It is proposed that this board should have placed at its disposal such resources as are necessary to make its action effective.

Thus we give to the Federal Farm Board every arm with which to deal with the multitude of problems. This is an entirely different method of approach to solution from that of a general formula; it is flexible and adaptable. No such far-reaching and specific proposal has ever been made by a political party on behalf of any industry in our history. It is a direct business proposition. It marks our desire for establishment of the farmer's stability and at the same time maintains his independence and individuality.

This plan is consonant with our American ideals to avoid the government operation of commercial business; for it places the operation upon the farmer himself, not upon a bureaucracy. It puts the government in its real relation to the citizen—that of co-operation. Its object is to give equality of opportunity to the farmer. I would consider it the greatest honor I could have if it should become my privilege to aid in finally solving this, the most difficult of economic problems presented to our people, and the one in which by inheritance and through long contact I have my deepest interest.

I am hopeful that in the December session of Congress it will be possible to reach that solution. However, as I have already said, if this is not possible I would call a special session in order that we might speedily arrive at a determination of the question before the next harvest.

The Principle of Co-operation

I have said that there is a third great group of activities in the promotion of the public welfare where the government, without abandoning the American system, may develop a new principle of relation with its citizens.

We have in the past quarter of a century evolved a higher sense of organized co-operation than has ever been known before. We have ten thousand examples of this conscious co-operative development in the enormous growth of associational activities. Civic associations, chambers of commerce, trade associations, professional associations, labor unions, trade councils, farm organizations, farm co-operatives, welfare associations—these are so all-embracing that there is scarcely an individual in our country who does not now belong to one or more of them. They represent every phase of our national life both on the economic and on the welfare side. They constitute a vast ferment toward conscious co-operation. They have become a part of the very fabric of American life. While some of them engage in highly objectionable attempts to wrongly influence public opinion and the action of government, the majority of them recognize a responsibility to the public as well as to themselves; and a large part of them are founded solely on public interest.

Wherever these associations undertake high public purposes I wish to see active co-operation by the government with them. Without intrusion the government can serve to bring together discordant elements and to secure co-operation between different industries and groups. It gives great hope of a new basis of solution for many of our problems and progressive action in our people. It should be the response of government to our new economic conceptions. It is consonant with the American system. It is a method that reinforces our individualism by reducing, and not increasing, government interference in business and the life of our citizens.

Such co-operation strengthens the whole foundations

of self-government and serves to maintain equality of opportunity and constructive leadership.

This co-operation can take two distinct directions. It can assist in the promotion of constructive projects of public interest on one hand, and it can assist in the cure of abuses by the voluntary establishment of a higher code of ethics and a stricter standard in the conduct of business.

Its Application in the Department of Commerce

These are not theoretical proposals. Seven and one-half years ago I introduced this relationship between the Department of Commerce and industrial, commercial, and civic organizations of our country for the promotion of matters that were of public importance. We co-operated with these associational groups in promotion of foreign trade, in the elimination of waste, in furtherance of economic and scientific research, in improvement of homes, and in scores of other activities. During this period hundreds of committees have been in active co-operation with the Department of Commerce, not under compulsion and not even under solicitation from the Department, but merely because the government was willing and ready to assist in bringing together the elements of any movement that would promote public welfare. I perhaps may make my proposals more clear by giving you some illustrations.

First, I may review a case of assistance to labor and business. In 1923, under my chairmanship, there was organized a series of committees representing the manufacturers, contractors, engineers, real estate men, and labor in the building trades. Its purpose was to reduce the loss of time due to the seasonal character of these industries. As a result of the organization set up, the average winter unemployment in these trades has been reduced from about one hundred days to about half that number. There has been no decrease in daily wages. The annual income of the workers in these trades has been substantially increased by the decrease in idle days, and the business given greater stability.

Another instance of action of fundamental importance to the farmer, the business man, and the worker consists of the measures taken in co-operation between the government and business agencies to mitigate the violence of the so-called business cycle. Booms and slumps have occurred periodically for one hundred years. No one suffers more from these periodic hard times, with their hideous unemployment, decrease in wages, and bankruptcy in business, than both labor and the farmers. Time forbids a discussion of the intricate problems involved and the remedies which have been inaugurated. The proof of their effectiveness lies in the fact that we have had a far longer period of stability in industry and commerce, far greater security in employment, and larger buying power for farm products than ever before in our history. The solution of this question was just as intricate as those which we face in agriculture.

Still another instance of these activities and one in which I have felt great concern has been the effort to build up safeguards for the independent business man. The preservation of his independence and individuality is just as important as maintaining the individuality of our farmers. Through various co-operative measures we have made a start to give to the independent business man many of the services of bigger business aggregations.

Avoidance of Unnecessary Regulation

An illustration of another direction of these activities has been in eliminating abuses in a particular industry without resort to legislation and regulation. For a great many years legislation had been debated in Congress providing for the regulation of the lumber industry somewhat on the lines of the pure food laws, in order to protect the honest manufacturers and dealers and the public. In 1923, however, we created a series of committees amongst associations in the lumber industry at their request. In the course of a gradual extension over five years we finally perfected a system for the grading of lumber and for the guaranteeing of these grades to the public, which is now carried out wholly within and by the lumber industry itself. Consequently during these last few years there has been no suggestion of such legislation from Congress. The savings to the public in the elimination of waste and fraud have been estimated by the industry as upwards of two hundred and fifty million dollars a year. This is a clear case where by co-operative methods we have avoided the necessity of regulation with the bureaucracy and interference that flow from it. It is also a clear case of building up of self-government.

I could describe a great number of such co-operative actions carried through to success. They involve such things as the Better-Homes movement, with its five thousand committees covering every city and village in the United States, engaged in promoting home ownership and betterment of home construction. They involve the American Child Health Association, which has been built up to bring about co-operation between national, state, and institutional health authorities for the promotion of better health surroundings for our children. I could relate to you at great length the vast co-operative machinery we have erected for the promotion of foreign trade, through which the growth of our trade has outstripped that of any country in the world.

In this broad field of co-operation by government lie potentialities which have been barely touched. The government can give leadership and co-operation. It can furnish scientific research. It can give prestige and influence. All of these call for but trivial expenditures. They require no increased bureaucracy. They are of first importance to every branch of American life.

It is by this means of co-operation by the government that we contribute mightily toward business stability and greater productivity in industry. And it is stability that every business man needs that he may thus work out for himself his own destiny without those ill tides over which he has no control.

It is by means of this sort of co-operation from the government that we may contribute greatly to the very foundations of economic progress, that is, to provide continuous and full employment. General employment comes not only with sound policies of government but equally from vigorous co-operation by the government to promote economic welfare. It is by these means that we can build such organization of our economic system as to provide a job for all who have the will to work.

Applies Also to Agriculture

I believe we can apply to agriculture the principles and activities in this direction which we have applied to commerce and industry during the last seven and one-half years. I believe we can solve a very large number of the problems of agricultural distribution and marketing through such methods. To that end I wish to have an effort made to secure the co-ordinated action of all of those interested in the distribution of farm products. I look forward to the day when our farm organizations will be as co-operatively and as advantageously linked to governmental encouragement and service as many of our industrial organizations are now.

It is from this co-operation of government with the great agencies of public welfare that we may inspire and build up the contributions to stronger family life, better homes, more recreation, and general well-being.

Facing a New Epoch

Before I conclude I should like to review to you some thoughts on the broader issues which we have before us.

For several years we were engaged in war. Since its close we have devoted ourselves largely to reconstruction of the losses from it. We have now entered upon the period of constructive action.

Equality of Opportunity

Government has the definite and manifest obligation of giving constructive leadership to the people. In doing so it must not lessen their initiative and enterprise, upon which we must rely for the progress of the race and of the nation. Our system has been built upon the ideal of equality of opportunity. For perhaps a hundred years after the foundation of the Republic, the opportunities of a moving frontier preserved that equality of opportunity. Now with the settlement of the country and with the astonishing speed and intricate complexity of industrial life, the preservation of equality of opportunity becomes yearly and yearly more difficult, and for that very reason is of higher and higher importance. If we would maintain America as the land of opportunity, where every boy and girl may have the chance to climb to that position to which his ability and character entitle him, we shall need to be on increasing guard. If I could drive the full meaning and importance of maintained equality of opportunity into the very consciousness of the American people, I would feel I had made some contribution to American life. It is the most precious of our possessions that the windows of every home shall look out upon unlimited hope. Equality of opportunity is the right of every American, rich or poor, foreign or native born, without respect to race or religion. By its maintenance alone can we hold open the door of full achievement to every new generation and to every boy and girl. Only from confidence that this right will be upheld can flow that unbounded courage and hope which stimulates each individual man and woman to endeavor and to accomplishment. By this principle we should test every act of government, every proposal, whether it be economic or political. I insist upon the most strict regulation of public utilities, because otherwise they would destroy equality of opportunity. I object to the government going into business in competition with its citizens because that would destroy equality of opportunity. And equality of opportunity is the flux with which alone we can melt out full and able leadership to the nation.

The first step to maintained equality of opportunity amongst our people is, as I have said before, that there should be no child in America who has not been born, and who does not live, under sound conditions of health; who does not have full opportunity for education from the kindergarten to the university; who is not free from injurious labor; who does not have stimulation to ambition to the fullest of his or her capacities. It is a matter of concern to our government that we should strengthen the safeguards to health. These activities of helpfulness and of co-operation stretch before us in every direction. A single generation of Americans of such a production would prevent more of crime and of illness, and give more of spirit and of progress than all of the repressive laws and police we can ever invent—and it would cost less.

The American Home

I have said often before in this campaign that we need always to interpret our discussions of economic and material proposals by how they affect the peace, the happiness, and the security and prosperity of every American home. I have tried to interpret to my fellow-countrymen what government means to that home. I stand for a prosperous country because I want good homes. You cannot divide those things that are seen from those that are unseen. The things that we call material are the foundation stones upon which we build the temple of those things that we call spiritual. Prosperity, security, happiness, and peace rest on sound economic life. Many of the subjects with which we have had to deal are intricate and complex. We must support the maintenance of peace amongst nations, economy in government, the protective tariff, the restriction of immigration, the encouragement of foreign trade, the relief of agriculture, the building of waterways, and a score of other great governmental policies which affect every home in our land. Solution of these questions is not always easy. Only the inexperienced can be positive in offering solutions of great problems. The first necessity in the handling of such problems is the assembling of the facts in their proper perspective. The truth must be forged from the metal of facts.

Reply to Senator Moses Reaffirmed

Let me in closing repeat a part of my message to the Kansas City convention in reply to the telegram from its chairman. I said:

"You convey too great a compliment when you say

that I have earned the right to the presidential nomination. No man can establish such an obligation upon any part of the American people. My country owes me no debt. It gave me, as it gives every boy and girl, a chance. It gave me schooling, independence of action, opportunity for service and honor. In no other land could a boy from a country village, without inheritance or influential friends, look forward with unbounded hope.

"My whole life has taught me what America means. I am indebted to my country beyond any human power to repay. It conferred upon me the mission to administer America's response to the appeal of afflicted nations during the war. It has called me into the Cabinets of two Presidents. By these experiences I have observed the burdens and responsibilities of the greatest office in the world. That office touches the happiness of every home. It deals with the peace of nations. No man could think of it except in terms of solemn consecration.

"A new era and new forces have come into our economic life and our setting among nations of the world. These forces demand of us constant study and effort if prosperity, peace, and contentment shall be maintained.

"You have manifested a deep concern in the problems of agriculture. You have pledged the party to support specific and constructive relief upon a nation-wide scale backed by the resources of the Federal Government. We must and will find a sound solution that will bring security and contentment to this great section of our people.

"But the problems of the next four years are more than economic. In a profound sense they are moral and spiritual.

"Shall the world have peace? Shall prosperity in this nation be more thoroughly distributed? Shall we build steadily toward the ideal of equal opportunity to all our people? Shall there be secured that obedience to law which is the essential assurance of the life of our institutions? Shall honesty and righteousness in government and in business confirm the confidence of the people in their institutions and in their laws?

"Government must contribute to leadership in answer to these questions. The government is more than administration; it is power for leadership and co-operation with the forces of business and cultural life in city, town, and countryside. The Presidency is more than executive responsibility. It is the inspiring symbol of all that is highest in America's purposes and ideals."

In that spirit I began this campaign. In that spirit I end it.

Mr. Hoover closed the campaign with a brief address, delivered, as were most of his campaign addresses, over a nation-wide radio hook-up, this time from the study of his home on San Juan Hill, Stanford University.

PALO ALTO, CALIFORNIA

November 5, 1928

I HAVE been asked to speak this last night before election directly to the vast radio audience of the United States. I shall not discuss partisan questions, nor shall I speak for more than a few moments on this occasion. I have endeavored to make clear during this campaign the principles, views, and ideals which are advocated by my party and myself.

I wish to emphasize that great function of American citizenship which every one of us should perform tomorrow. The ballot is the most sacred individual act in that great system of self-government which we have inherited and which it is our duty to carry forward. It is the direct opportunity for every man and woman to assert a direct personal influence upon the kind of national government and the policies which he wishes pursued during the next four years.

It is estimated that over forty-two million men and women have registered in preparation for casting their ballots. This registration exceeds by twelve or fifteen million any previous registration in the history of our country. This is to a great extent due to our women, who are alive to the fact that the issues in national elections more seriously than ever before affect every home in our country. Women have achieved their rights at the ballot; they have now accepted their responsibilities.

In my public statements I have earnestly urged that there rested upon government many responsibilities which affect the moral and spiritual welfare of our people. The participation of women in elections has produced a keener realization of the importance of these questions and has contributed to higher national ideals. Moreover, it is through them that our national ideals are ingrained in our children.

Never before in the history of the world have forty millions of people of any commonwealth prepared to express their convictions and determination as to the character of government of their country and the future policies which they desire to see adopted and carried out. It is the greatest spectacle and the greatest inspiration in self-government that has ever been witnessed in the whole history of the world. It should hearten the confidence of every believer in government by the people.

This enormously enlarged interest is evidence of the great depth of conviction and even anxiety of our people over this momentous decision. And whatever that decision is, it will be right. I believe in the will of the majority. It represents the common will and conscience of our people.

Our two great political parties have laid before you their principles and policies. And I am a believer in party government. It is only through party organization that our people can give coherent expression to their views on great issues which affect the welfare and future of the Republic. There is no other way. Furthermore, it is only through party organization that we may fix the responsibility for the assured execution of these promises. Our national campaigns are a period of renewed consideration of the fundamentals which make for progress and for prosperity, that make for moral and spiritual advancement. We are a nation of progressives; we differ as to what is the road to progress.

I differ widely with many of the principles and views advocated by our opponents and the proposals which they have put forward. But it is not my purpose to review these questions. We are, or should be, a nation of individuals, and should make independent determination of our conclusions. Democracy cannot survive if the ballot is to be cast upon somebody's order or direction. Democracy in such a state would become the destroyer of liberty, and not its guarantee.

It is contrary to our national ideals that any party should represent any section of our country, and this election, more than any that has gone before, gives hope for the breaking down of sectional lines. There ought no longer to be any North, South, East, or West in our national thought. Our ideals as Americans have been molded and welded under leadership of men and women from every section of our country. The greatest progress can come in advancement of our institutions, our ideas, and our ideals by the common contribution of every section.

We shall have with us this year millions of first voters. I wish to express welcome to them. We welcome them to the common task of building a better and better social order and the welding of idealism of youth into political life.

This election is of more momentous order than for many years because we have entered into a new era of economic and moral action, not only in our country but in the world at large. Our national task is to meet our many new problems, and in meeting them to courageously preserve our rugged individualism, together with the principles of ordered liberty and freedom, equality of opportunity, with that idealism to which our nation has been consecrated and which has brought us to the leadership of the world.

The American voting booth is the place where every ballot should be lodged upon the conviction of each individual as to the principles and issues of the party which will best serve the future of America. It is only by this consecrated independence of judgment that we may truly give expression to the will of a great people. Therefore, I urge upon each citizen to vote, and vote early, and to vote seriously and earnestly as conscience and mind direct.

And before I close, I wish to express my gratitude to the millions of men and women who have given to our cause their support and labor during these months. Any American may be proud to have been chosen their leader.

Good night, my friends.

STATEMENT TO PRESS AFTER ELECTION

November 7, 1928

I CAN make no adequate expression of gratitude for the overwhelming confidence of our people, who, without regard to section or interest, have selected me for President of the whole United States. There has been a vindication of great issues and a determination of the true road of progress. The Republican Party has again been assessed with a great responsibility. In this hour there can be for me no feeling of victory or exultation. Rather it imposes a sense of solemn responsibility for the future and of complete dependence upon Divine guidance for the task which the greatest office in the world imposes. That task is to give the best within me to interpret the common sense and the ideals of the American people. I can only succeed in my part by the co-operation and unity of spirit of all leaders of opinion and of action for the common service of our country.

INDEX

Abuses, 29; correction of, 198

Acceptance, address of, 9, 72, 80, 149

Administration, Republican, 58, 66, 70, 73; achievements of, 65 f., 74, 108, 120, 121

Aeroplane, 98

Agriculture, 102 f., 188 f.; aids to, 151; basis has shifted, 51; building of industry in, 185; causes for failure, 18; control of, 53; co-operatives and pools, 19, 53; cost of transportation, 186; dependent on foreign markets, 99; disaster in, 127; factors in solution of problem, 191 f.; increase in, 117; industry lagged, 13, 173; and labor, 76; larger units of, 19; methods applied to, 23; milestones of changes, 50; modern business operations of, 53; in New England, 110 f.; not under government control, 53; not one industry, 18, 51, 190; not subsidize, 53; problems of, 4 f., 17, 22, 54, 188, 189, 194 f., 207; problems unsolved, 190; prostrated after war, 12; protective tariff for, 128; rehabilitation of, 58; security of earlier days not desirable, 51 f.; social problem, 190 f.; solution of some problems, 202; some branches recovered, 18; sound marketing organization, 53; Southern, 102, 110 f.; specialization in, 52; stability and prosperity of, 173;

transformation in, 52; waterways and, 55, 56, 57; *see* Farm relief

Alabama, 89

American Child Health Association, 201

American system, the 152 f., 154, 155, 156, 163, 165, 167 f., 173, 175, 179, 181, 196, 197

Anarchy, 42

Appointive offices, 106

Arbitration, 39

Arena, Boston, 114

Argentine, 55

Arkansas River, 184

Armistice, 12

Army, 40, 105

Associations, civic, 32, 78, 196 f.

Atlantic Ocean, 20, 21, 56, 57, 184

Aunt Hannah, 49

Australia, 55

Automobiles, 15, 65, 70, 82, 93, 98, 99, 119, 169

Aviation, development of, 43, 151

Balance of trade, international, 133

Ballot, 35, 64, 129, 211–214

Bank clearings in South, 94; *see* Savings deposits

Banking, 82

Bankruptcy, periods of, 34, 79, 199

Barter, 132, 133

Belgian Relief, 4, 207

Belgium, buying power of, 69

Benefit societies, 70

Better-Homes Association, 94, 201

Boom and slump, 33, 77, 79, 188, 199

219

Employment (*Continued*):
on government policies, 64, 70; diversity of, 57; effect of Underwood tariff, 71; full, 83, 202; organization of, 175; restoration of, 151; stability of, 4, 23, 63 f., 80, 121; *see* Unemployment

Equal opportunity, 5, 41, 58, 59, 86, 153, 163, 165, 175, 180, 188, 197, 203, 204 f., 208, 214; Abraham Lincoln stood for, 42; in American system, 181; in business, 42, 166; to farmer, 196; for farmers' children, 25, 54; fundamental principle of nation, 42, 168, 214; legislation to provide, 106; Midwest has not had, 183; *see* Opportunity

Equality: the ideal of, 40 f.; economic, 102; *see* Equal opportunity

Essex County, New Jersey, 62

Europe, 65, 98, 136, 138, 155; *see* Buying power, War debts

Experience, 128, 129, 132, 134, 179

Exports, 13, 74, 82; expansion of trade, 118; of foreign countries, 75; increase in, 129; in 1922, 74; in 1927, 74 f., 121; trade not ruined by tariff, 138

Family, 14, 17, 60, 66, 75, 82, 86, 100, 102, 194

Farm: co-operatives, acts supporting, 21; electrical power for, 111; more than a business, 19, 190; occupations of, now conducted in factory, 52; prices, 128; problems, 21; small, 142; *see* Farm relief

Farm relief, 206; constructive measures, 23; definite plan of, 22; farmer-controlled stabilization, 195; pledged to, 196, 207; problems of, 155; program of, 53 f., 156; proposals for, 194 f.; tariff the foundation of, 20; vital method of, 20, 21; waterways necessary for, 55

Farmer, 24; acts to aid, 103; added markets, 75; benefit of tariff policy for, 20, 127; buying power, 73; diminished market, 142; economically free, 191; efficiency of, 99, 188 f.; engages in destructive competition, 19; export of products, 74; freight paid by, 55; income for, 23, 51, 54; losses to, 18, 24, 53; to maintain individuality, 35, 53, 103, 195; market better in U.S., 122; no tax for stabilization, 103; prices to, 56, 79; production increased, 189; protection of standards of living, 4, 151; security of home of, 118; surplus sold abroad, 73, 120; tariff protects, 102; units of production must not be large, 19; wife of, 23, 54

Federal Farm Banks, 189

Federal Farm Board, 21, 53, 103, 194, 195

Federal Government, 5, 12, 22, 23, 28, 80 f., 106 f., 111, 122, 152, 158, 159, 164, 183, 207; *see* Government

Financial stability, 34

Fishing, 48, 170

Flax, growers, 24; tariff for, 192

Flood control, 27–29, 104 f., 107, 164, 183, 186

Foreign countries, buying power of, 69, 132, 134, 135, 138

Foreign debts, 12, 13, 135

Foreign markets, 20, 34, 55, 56, 72, 77, 99, 111; routes to, 143; *see* Transportation *and* Markets

Foreign monopolies, 123, 124

Foreign relations, 64

Foreign trade, 73 ff., 117, 119, 122, 151, 198, 206; affected by tariff, 115, 132, 137; after Armistice, 12; not barter, 133; co-operative machinery for, 201; development of, 105, 117; increasing, 97, 136; "invisibles" of, 134; merchant marine necessary, 140; New England and, 116 f.; promotion of, pledged, 4, 34, 43, 105, 120, 124; safeguarding, 124; stimulant to employment, 75 f.; and war debts, 137; and world prosperity, 126

Foreign wages, 127

France, 69, 131

Free speech, 162, 163

Free-trade theories, 132

Freight, 55, 134, 183, 188; *see* Transportation

Fremont, General, 92

Frontiers, 89, 204

Fruit growers, 24, 192

"Full dinner pail," 27, 169

Garfield, President, 49

Georgia, 92

Germany, 69, 131

Gompers, Samuel, 160 f.

Government: bureaus, 32; and business, 30, 31, 65, 84, 100, 106 ff., 120, 153, 155, 157, 158 f., 162 f., 164, 174, 196, 197; centralization of, 154; children dependent upon, 38; competition with business, 31, 181, 205; confidence in form of, 14; conflicting ideas of, 10–11; constructive, 179 ff., 182; control of rates, 166; co-operation with business, 152, 173; co-operation with employers, 66, 70, 74; creation of public works, 164; economy in, 4; expenditure, 33; and flood control, 107; fundamental principles of, 149; leadership from, 5; and navigation, 107; operation of railways, 160; party, 213; of people, 108; policies of, 32, 67, 95; promotion of business a function of, 33 f.; regulation of business, 31, 165 f., 200; righteousness and honesty, 5; and scientific research, 107; *see* Federal Government *and* Co-operation

Government ownership, competition with business, 22, 106, 107, 111, 141; of hydro-electric power, 156; for merchant marine, tried, 141; not efficient, 141; not favored, 107; Samuel Gompers on, 160 f.; in war time, 154

Grain exchanges, 189

Great Britain, wages in, 131

Great Lakes, 20 f., 57

Great War, 4, 10, 12, 18, 38, 55, 56, 67, 68, 73 f., 97, 112, 119, 120, 126, 132, 137, 139, 150, 153 f., 168 f., 203

Gulf of Mexico, 21, 57, 143, 184

Hard wheat, 192

Harmon Field, 88

Home: American, of the New Day, 176, 205 f.; assure, against unemployment, 101; burden of armament upon, 40; comforts in farmer's, 23, 52; for development of child, 38; drudgery saved, 170; electricity in, 14; farm is a, 190; fuller life to,

Home (*Continued*):
115; happiness of, 4; improvement in American, 16, 60, 198; ownership of, 14, 201; security in, 118; small, suffers from tariff changes, 143; in South, 93; tariff and the, 24; unit of American life, 100; windows to look on unlimited hope, 204
Homes: better, 70, 111, 151, 169, 203; happier, 44; nation of, 11, 60; purchasing power of, 65, 79; *see* Better Homes Association
Hoover, Andrew, 92
Housing, 175
Houston, Sam, 92
Hydro-electric power, 27, 28, 64, 77, 155, 156, 164; *see* Electrical power

Ideals, 84, 86, 89, 90
Illinois River, to be deepened, 56
Immigrants, remittances by, 134, 135
Immigration, 24, 25, 71 f., 98, 104, 151, 194, 206
Imports: bulk admitted free, 133; of farm products, 191; increase of, 121 f., 136; material, 118, 123; of tropical products, 119
Income: annual, 79; in building trades, 199; family, of interest to women, 115; in homes, 105; reduction of, 128; taxes of, 13
Indiana, 65
Individual, equality of, 41
Individual initiative, 4
Individualism, ideal of, 41 f.
Industry, 52, 65, 80; *see* Labor
Infant mortality reduced, 170
Inflation, 66, 139
Initiative, 60, 84, 153, 154; individual, 159, 163, 180
Injunction, use of, 27, 83

Inland waterways, 20, 21, 43, 54 f., 56, 98, 104, 111, 151, 183, 184, 185, 206
Institutions of higher learning, 15
Insurance, 15, 70, 82, 93, 134, 170; *see* Life insurance
Integrity, American, 58, 109, 110; of business men, 31
Intermediate Credit Banks, 189
International balances, 133
International law, 39
International relations, 39, 98
Inventions, 163; new, 31, 51, 70, 99, 116; promotion of, 34
"Invisibles" of foreign trade, 134
Iowa, 50 f., 58
Irrigation, 27, 28, 43, 164
Italy, buying power, 69

Jackson, President Andrew, 167
Japan, buying power, 69

Kansas, decreased prices in, 143
Kansas City, 10, 56, 184; convention, 206
Kentucky, 92, 101
Kings Mountain, 91; Battle of, 88

Labor: and agriculture, 76; American, 73, 76; assistance to, 199; benefits of union, 26; British, 76; capital and, 180; conflicts, 77; co-operation of, 25; disputes, injunction in, 27; Gompers and, 161; hours of, 15, 68, 69, 170; interests of, 25; machines for hand, 117; pledge to support of, 27; present situation of, 66; products of, 74; protection of, 64; safety of, 70; unions, 197; unity of, and other interests, 76; and wages, 64
Labor-saving devices, 72, 76, 83; *see* Inventions

Tariff, 20, 101, 115, 117, 192; and buying power of foreign countries, 135; foundation of farm relief, 20; and imports, 129; inadequate to protect farmer, 18, 65, 191; an issue, 126 f.; protective, 24, 70 f., 101 f., 128, 151, 189, 192 f., 206; reduction would injure homes, 24, 115; revision of laws, 25, 129 f.; and wages, 131, 193; see Underwood Tariff Act

Tariff act, of 1922, 102, 129, 136

Taxation, 34, 159

Taxes, 98; income, 13; increased local, 18; reduction of, 13, 43, 105, 124, 151; war, 139

Taylor, Alfred A., 88, 96

Taylor, "Fiddlin' Bob," 88, 96

Telephones, 15, 82, 93, 119

Tennessee, 88, 89, 92, 96

Tennessee River, 184

Texas, 92

Textile industry, 13, 68, 102, 130 ff., 142, 173

Theory, see Experience

Thompson, Charles, 9

Tourists, 134, 135, 138

Trade: not barter, 133; polyangular course of, 13

Trade union movement, 26

Tramp steamers, 140

Transportation, 27, 28, 64, 65, 77, 98, 104, 186, 191; see Inland waterways and Freight

Treaties, renouncing war, 39

Tremont Temple, 114

Tropical goods, 118, 119, 123, 133, 138

Uharrie River farm, 92

Uncle Allen, 50

Underwood Tariff, 71, 188; Bill, 127, 128, 193

Unemployment, 12, 15, 63 f., 67, 81, 120; assure home against, 101, 104; in building trades, 199; collective bargaining and, 64; diminishing, 67 f., 79, 151, 169; in 1921, 66, 67; periods of, 34, 79 f., 80; public works to relieve, 28; seasonal, 77, 78, 79, 187; see Employment

United Kingdom, buying power, 69

United States, buying power, 69; fundamental principles of, 149; government, biggest business, 107

Vegetable oils, 192

Vermont, 89

Veterans, relief of, 105, 151

Virginia, 91

Voters, first, 214

Wage earners, 80

Wages: American, 73, 75, 76, 128, 131; bargaining for, 161; in building trades, 199; fictitious, 168; and government, 64; high, 68, 69, 76, 81, 118; increase in, 160, 169; and the labor unions, 26, 64; lower, cause diminished market, 142; and machinery, 82; of Midwest, 193; and prosperity, 26, 66; in 1921, 66; purchasing power of, 15; in South, 93; and standards of living, 26, 63, 66, 72, 135; in textile industry, 131

Wall Street, 142

War debts, 98, 132, 137 f., 139, 150, 153 f., 168 f., 203

War Finance Corporation, 189

Washington, George, 9

Waste, 23, 27 f., 34, 76, 77 f., 105, 132, 142, 191, 195, 198, 201

13465